The Meaning of Pastoral Care

The Meaning of
PASTORAL CARE

By Carroll A. Wise

Published expressly for Garrett-Evangelical Theological
Seminary through the generosity of Mr. Peter Volid for
the Carroll A. Wise Scholarship Fund.

HARPER & ROW, PUBLISHERS

New York, Hagerstown, San Francisco, London

To those persons to whom I have been privileged to stand in a relationship of pastoral care, and to those students with whom I have been privileged to enter into a mutual teaching-learning relationship

Contents

Introduction

Certain problems in pastoral care have been emerging during the past four decades, whether the setting has been a parish, a hospital, or a theological seminary. Perhaps the central problem has been this: What does pastoral care have to offer persons, and how is it given? There has been some real questioning of the value of offering the intellectual, liturgical, and ecclesiastical structures of religion in certain circumstances, and there have been answers pro and con. Some theologians have joined pastors in asserting the value of offering theological ideas as part of pastoral care. But the real question has remained. How and under what conditions do the various structures of religion become meaningful to persons?

This book is not an attempt to do away with the structures of religion. Obviously that would be foolishness. It is an attempt to show that structures are undergirded by a deeper element, an element which has often been called spirit. This book cuts across certain traditional approaches and elaborates the conviction that relationships are fundamental to pastoral care. This has been a neglected dimension, but it appears to be the basis for dealing with certain pressing questions. Although relationship is often casually assumed, and then lightly dismissed, it is at once the desperate need of persons and the essential quality of the Gospel. Many questions in pastoral care are hardly intelligible unless one is constantly aware of the distinction between the structures of the faith and relationships within the faith, and understands on which level he is thinking. The emphasis of this book is on the meaning of pastoral relationships as the basis for the communication of the Gospel.

This book is also an attempt to relate the theological dimension of pastoral care to the personal dimension. Because of the nature of the problems involved, one can go only so far with verbal formulations. I make no claim to have gone the limit. However, I would stress the idea that any real integration of the two dimensions occurs within the person of the pastor when form and spirit find a workable and working unity in the depths of his being.

As the title indicates, this is not a work on the techniques of pastoral care. It is rather an attempt to interpret the meaning of pastoral care, and to set pastoral care within the context of the Gospel. To the extent that this book has grasped the real issues and processes, it will have contributed a basis for judging techniques. The emphasis is more on the dimensions of being and knowing, in the direct personal sense, than of doing.

The concept of pastoral care elaborated here is more inclusive than the usual one which confines pastoral care to dealing with persons in certain kinds of life crises. The concern is with pastoral care in relation to the growth of persons, and with the psychological aspects of growth in relation to pastoral care. Genuine pastoral care in today's world cannot afford to be otherwise.

This book owes much to more people than I can at any moment consciously bring to mind. Teachers, colleagues, and students have contributed much. Above all, I am indebted to persons with whom I have stood in the pastoral relationship. It has been my privilege to give portions of the book as lectures in conferences for pastors, in theological seminaries, and to groups of laymen. I have profited from their reactions and comments. More specifically I would like to express appreciation for the intellectual encounters and personal fellowship which have come through membership in the faculty of the Garrett Theological Seminary. This is a stimulating relationship in which to live and work, made all the more so by the cross-fertilization of inquisitive students who carry pollen from one professorial mind to another, to the enrichment of all. Two of my colleagues, Dr. William Hordern and Dr. Morris Taggart, have read parts of the manuscript and have given valuable suggestions.

One person whom I wish to mention in gratitude is Dr. Anton

T. Boisen, not because he is the source of any of the ideas in this book, though he may be, but rather because he started me on a long experience of clinical pastoral training. He constantly insisted that his students learn to read the human document.

My thanks to Miss Marilyn Butt who efficiently put the manuscript into final form. And my gratitude to my wife, Addiene G. Wise, for constant inspiration and support.

CARROLL A. WISE

April, 1966

The Biblical Basis of Pastoral Care

THE living model of pastoral care for the Christian minister is the person and work of Jesus as revealed in the Gospels. Abstract concepts of pastoral care have been developed through the centuries under such labels as "pastoral theology," but these concepts have been powerless to create effective pastors. A Christian pastor is one who in his very person and in his living relationships with people mediates something of the quality of being which is found in a larger measure in the revelation of Christ. This quality of being speaks, in turn, of a quality in the eternal nature of God, and of a living relationship which God offers men. Because it is a gift of God to men, its manifestation in human life speaks of the Giver. In this living relationship there are reconciliation, forgiveness, and healing which reach below the struggles of human existence into the very core of man's being. Out of this relationship come insight and power for daily life. This living relationship is the context in which the Holy Spirit manifests itself. Only the presence of the Holy Spirit will save a pastor from a mechanical imitation of the model presented by Jesus—with all of the destructiveness of such imitation.

We cannot here review all of the material in the New Testament out of which a Christian conception of pastoral care develops.[1] The charge which Jesus gave his disciples prior to sending them out on a mission is clear (Matt. 9:35–10:16). They were persons sent in his name, with his authority, to carry on his mission and ministry. They were to preach that the Kingdom of God was a present potentiality waiting to be realized in the lives of men. They were to heal the sick, raise the dead, cleanse the lepers, cast out demons. In other words, they were to deal with the profound needs of human beings as they had seen Jesus dealing with those needs. As the disciples had received, so they were to give, freely and in the spirit of their Master. The principle involved here is very important. The pastor cannot give unless he has first received. Indeed, giving and receiving are simultaneous experiences, and pastoral care is a deeply mutual undertaking.

The origin of the pastoral concept in the ancient art of shepherding is well known. In John 10 Jesus is reported to have used the symbol as a vehicle for the interpretation of his mission, and consequently for the work of those whom he sent out. Seward Hiltner[2] has recently elaborated this concept. However, this symbol cannot have the power for modern men which it had in the first century. There are other symbols more realistic to the modern mind. While recognizing the power of this symbol as Jesus used it, we shall not make much use of it in this study, but shall attempt to deal with the realities involved in the care of the pastor for his people. One of the dangers of this symbol to the modern mind is that it can subtly but powerfully convey the idea of the superiority of the pastor over his "sheep," whereas in the New Testament, pastoral care is the ministry of a person who stands in the same relationship to God as do the persons to whom he ministers.

A symbol more meaningful and powerful to modern men is that which St. Paul uses in II Corinthians 5. Here the stress is on the experience of reconciliation: God through Christ has reconciled us to Himself and has given us the ministry of reconciliation. Today men are aware of conflict on many levels—personal, social, ideational, political—and of the need for reconciliation. Indeed, a new profession has been developed, that of psychotherapy, aimed at helping persons resolve inner conflict and become reconciled, at least in part, to themselves and to others. Throughout this book, we shall stress the goal of reconciliation as fundamental to pastoral care.

A final New Testament passage to which we would call attention is to be found in I Corinthians 12:4–13:13. The burden of this passage is first of all the charismatic nature of the ministry. It is the exercise of gifts through the Spirit, and there are different gifts corresponding to the different functions which need to be fulfilled in the Church. But there is only one Spirit, the same Lord and God "who inspires them all in everyone." Usually the thirteenth chapter is not seen as an integral part of Paul's discussion of the ministry. But if read as a whole, without regard to the mechanics of chapter and verse, it becomes clear that Paul is pointing to a higher gift which is indispensable in any form of the ministry, and that is the gift of love. Whether this be exegesis or eisegesis, New Testament scholars will have to decide. It is true to the reality of the Christian ministry, as we shall stress in the pages ahead. For whether a man preach, teach, conduct the affairs of the Church, or engage in any other pastoral activity, if he has not love his ministry is nothing. This is the central problem of the pastoral ministry today.

The ministry of our Lord as recorded in the New Testament was deep, inclusive, and richly varied. For this reason there is no one symbol that fully interprets his ministry. Today there is great stress on Christ as the Word of God, and hence on the ministry of the Word. This is often taken to be preaching. But Christ as the Word of God implies something far more than preaching. It points to a message revealed in a life which was grounded in a profound faith in God and in a self-giving love toward men. It was a communication from God to man on a level far deeper than the verbal—the level of being. The ministry of the Word is no less a pastoral ministry than it is a preaching ministry. It is far more than the spoken word. It is manifest or frustrated in the very life of the pastor as he comes into living contact with other persons.

Much of the pastoral ministry is in listening, not in speaking or preaching. But listening in understanding love is no less a ministry of the Word of Love than is proclaiming the love of God from the pulpit. Indeed, preaching, except for persons with inhibition of speech, is far easier and entails less personal stress than the ministry to individuals in time of deep need. This is one reason why so many "preachers" do so little and such poor work with individuals. Had Jesus not listened to many persons with understanding love and had he not reflected deeply on what he heard, it is difficult to see how he could have created the parables, which hold up a mirror before men so that those who have eyes may see themselves as God sees them.

As a textbook on pastoral care, the Gospel record is both com-

plete and incomplete. Much of what Jesus said and did is undoubtedly missing, much that we have is condensation, and
much undoubtedly has been distorted in transmission. The Gospels certainly cannot be considered a textbook on pastoral care in
any literal sense. There are problems encountered in pastoral
care on which they have nothing directly to say.

In another sense the Gospels are a complete revelation of the
meaning of pastoral care. This is because they reveal the Spirit of
Jesus in relation to persons and their needs. It is also because this
Spirit is in itself the manifestation of the Spirit of God. Jesus was
dedicated to showing forth the love of God in his own love for
people. "As the father has sent me, so send I you" (John 20:21)
was his charge to his disciples. Only he who has shared in this
ministry as a receiver will have any part of it to give.

The direction of the pastoral ministry of Jesus is as clear as its
source. It was directed to the needs of people. The full meaning
of this requires much reflection and elaboration.

Jesus was singularly free from one of the burdens of many
modern pastors—the task of maintaining an institution, or of
administering a church. One of the disillusionments of many
modern ministers is that they go into the ministry to help people,
but find themselves a part of the machinery of an institution in
which it seems they must use people rather than help them.
Richard Niebuhr's[3] description of the minister as a "pastoral-
director" is indicative of the schizophrenic split in the professional consciousness of many ministers today. Their personal
identity as ministers is anything but whole. Not so with Jesus. He
was free to minister to persons. Today there are movements
within the ministry which are seeking to learn how to use the
Church for the welfare of people, to learn how individuals may
be helped through the fellowship of the Church, and to see the
Church itself as an institution which should minister rather than
be ministered to. The Spirit which motivates the true pastor will
always be in conflict with that spirit which glorifies the institution and makes it an end in itself.

Jesus was also singularly free from the role problems[4] of the
modern pastor. This consciousness of role, the sense of conflict
and confusion of roles, the uncertainty as to what role should be
played and when, is again indicative of pathology within the

professional consciousness of the minister. He does not know who he is, therefore he does not know what role to play. The problem cannot be solved by playing a role, but only through that Spirit which informs any role. When one is primarily concerned with being a minister to persons, and sees any role only as a means to this end, he is putting Spirit and form in their proper relationship. Jesus had a real problem with the "role players" of his day, but he knew that regardless of the particular role in which daily events cast him, his task was to reveal the redemptive love of God to men. Even such an obviously "religious" discussion as worship soon got down to the deep needs of the man or woman to whom he was speaking. On one occasion he did such an unorthodox thing as calling down out of a tree a man who seemed to show more anxious need than those on the ground. The pastor who is clear on the matter of the inner spirit and purpose of his ministry has no problem with role.

Jesus was inwardly free for a redemptive ministry to persons. This was all that counted. This he saw as the fulfillment of the law and the prophets, but he opposed applications of the law when they interfered with the needs of persons. If persons were hungry or needed to be healed, he broke the law in regard to the Sabbath. To him, helping people was far more important than any status symbol. He mingled with publicans and sinners, he forgave harlots, and he discussed with Nicodemus the need to be reborn. His reach into the life that opened itself to him was deeper than any human manifestation of estrangement, and he died forgiving those who closed their hearts to him. Here was a man who could truly love the unlovable. This was the ministry of reconciliation, and it is to this ministry that the pastor is called. But to meet people in a redemptive love which places human values above all other values demands an inner freedom. It is difficult to come into the possession of such freedom.

At great cost to himself, Jesus gained freedom for a redemptive ministry even to those who hated and killed him. Whatever the depth of suffering out of which human bitterness and estrangement grow, Jesus plumbed that depth. He could express the utter isolation of suffering by the words, "My God, my God, why hast thou forsaken me?" Following this, he could experience a reunion with God in faith, and he could say, "Into thy hands I commit my spirit." The meaning of pastoral care is that we must be able to enter into and suffer with those whom we seek to help. If our concern to help others ends with those who require little cost on our own part, then we will not help many. The genuine pastor comes to his people as one who has taken their burden on himself, their suffering into himself. Not that he relieves them of their suffering, but in suffering with them and for them in love, he makes it possible for them to find the redemptive answer in love. The preaching of the Word of the Cross is but a futile gesture unless we are able to manifest that Word by taking suffering into ourselves. This means the ability to enter into deep empathy with others, feeling their pain, their anxiety, guilt and hate, but maintaining the integrity of the self in trust and love.

In the ministry of Jesus we see complete freedom from the human tendencies to exploit and manipulate. He was open and transparent before men, and therefore he could help men see themselves and what they were becoming and what they might become. Such openness is frightening to some men, and the frightened ones became Jesus' enemies because they saw that he would destroy in them what they were not ready to give up. His accessibility seemed to invite his friends to manipulate him into fulfilling their own image of him. This was the problem of Peter; but in Peter manipulativeness was finally mastered by a deeper and saving reality. The identity of Jesus was as a Servant of God, a suffering Servant who was to live out his mission concretely in the service of men, reaching into the depths of man's need and remaining personally and spiritually available to men. This is also an identity in which the modern pastor will find strength for his own ministry.

Finally, our ministry is *not our* ministry, but the continuation of Christ's ministry in us through his Spirit. The motive force of the pastoral ministry should not be our own problems or needs, although it is very difficult to eliminate these completely. The temptation in the ministry to work out various ego needs, to find disguised expression of sexual or hostile impulses, to project our own anxieties and guilts onto others, is very subtle, extensive, and potent. It is particularly dangerous because it operates un-consciously. There are strong forces at work within the personality of the pastor, as well as the person to whom he ministers, to keep certain needs out of awareness.

One way for the pastor to deal with this problem in himself is through the constant reminder that his ministry is not his private affair but is the ministry of Christ through him. Constant self-examination in the light of the Spirit of Christ as revealed in the Gospels, in relation to the specific persons to whom he ministers, should be a source of insight and growth. To meet another person in the name of Christ is not a merely formal relationship, nor is it a role to be played. "Inasmuch as you have done it unto one of the least of these, you have done it unto me" has profound spiritual implications for the pastoral ministry. The model for the Christian minister is not a formal one which he can imitate or follow to the letter. It is a living model of the Spirit, and this is the Spirit of Christ. It is in this Spirit that the true pastor fulfills his calling.

The Meaning of Pastoral Care

PASTORAL care is the art of communicating the inner meaning of the Gospel to persons at the point of their need. Thus pastoral care is not a theoretical discipline, although it may be undergirded by such disciplines as theology or Biblical interpretation. Pastoral care is not "pastoral theology," especially when this term denotes a set of principles for the conduct of a specific activity. Pastoral care is more a function than an activity, more a living relationship than a theory or interpretation, more a matter of being than of doing. It is the manifestation in the relationship between pastor and persons, either individually or in groups, of a quality of love which points to, and gives a basis in experience for, the realization of the love of God. The love of the pastor is not to be identified with the love of God, in that the pastor is weak, imperfect, and finite. But the pastor can be "with" a person in a manner which gives reality and meaning to the infinite love of God, or he may block the realization of that meaning. In a sense, any genuine human love is the manifestation of the love of God, since it is the gift of God shed abroad in our hearts through the Holy Spirit.

In the term "pastoral care" the word "care" expresses concern, and the word "pastoral" gives depth and direction to that concern. Thus pastoral care is distinctly different from "medical care." We have indicated, that the pastor's concern is rooted in the Gospel. As a Christian he is called to love others as God in Christ has loved him. As a Christian pastor he has special duties and responsibilities, and he should have specialized training to quality him for his work. In addition, he needs experiences which will develop his capacities for self-giving love.

Although the Gospel is the beginning and end of the pastor's ministry, he must also be concerned with the human factors which control or influence a person's perception of, and responses to, that Gospel. No human being receives and responds to the Gospel, either for the first time or after long experience within the Church, with pristine eyes and soul. He rather receives it against a background of ideas, feelings, and personality structures which predispose him to accept, reject, or distort the image and interpretation of Christ as found in the New Testament. These predisposing elements grow out of his experiences with other human beings in his family and in cultural relationships, and out of his responses to these relationships. These statements will receive some elaboration later. Here we must stress the principle that the genuine pastor is not satisfied to blame the rejection and distortion of the Gospel on the generalized idea of sin. He is concerned with the specific processes within the individual which give rise to his attitudes, and he understands that at least some of the effects of destructive experiences and relationships can be overcome by creative and redemptive relationships and processes. The genuine pastor sees himself as a medium of healing rather than of condemnation.

What is the Communication of the Gospel?

We have defined pastoral care as the communication of the Gospel to persons at the point of their need. Two obvious questions arise in any discussion of this concept. What is the Gospel which is to be communicated? And how is it communicated? Effective communication can take place only through means which can embody the reality to be communicated.

What is the Gospel? A full discussion of the content of the Gospel is obviously impossible here. The Christian pastor must have a thorough Biblical, theological, and historical training through which the elaboration of this question will take place. We are interested here in the nature of the Gospel as it bears on the kind of communication which is required in pastoral care.

The Gospel is usually described as the good news of God's redeeming love as revealed in Jesus Christ. The modern mind, saturated with the latest televised news reports, is likely to identify the Gospel with something which can be communicated by verbal and mechanical means. But the reality of the Gospel is something deeper than this. As Alan Richardson[1] says, "After the death and resurrection of Jesus the content of the Gospel, as it is understood by the Apostolic Church, is Christ himself." The Gospel, then, is a Person, and through this Person, a living relationship with God. The Gospel was embodied in a Person whose relationships with men have been taken to reveal the redemptive, reconciling relationship which God offers all men. In Jesus, God has taken the initiative in offering and demonstrating this relationship, and in Jesus the relationship was accepted and lived out. As men have responded, and still respond, in love and faith to Christ, they experience redemption or reconciliation with God. They are no longer separated and alienated and therefore lost. They experience the inner reality of God's acceptance of them as sons. This new relationship results in a new sense of being which enables them to move toward discovering and becoming the persons they are potentially. The suffering of Christ speaks of an aspect of the nature of God which reaches out to man on the level of his own deepest suffering, the anxiety caused by alienation from God. The Gospel is Christ himself and the power of the new relationship that God has offered to men through Christ.

This emphasis on the Gospel as a living relationship embodied in the person and work of Christ is pointedly expressed in the New Testament. The Pauline statement, "God was in Christ reconciling the world unto himself" (II Cor. 5:19) is one expression, and another is to be found in the Johannine phrase, "The Word became flesh and dwelt among us" (John 1:14). God's message to man concerning his redemptive love may be put into words, but the deepest and only fully adequate means of communication of God's love to men was its Incarnation in a Person and its expression in the relationship of that Person with other men in a historical setting. The idea of the Incarnation is not only a means of interpreting the meaning of Christ, but it also describes God's most effective means of communication with man. It is a demonstration in depth, a communication through Being, on a level far deeper than the verbal. Christ is indeed the "Word of God," but often we slip unconsciously into the human

error of confusing our words about Christ with the reality of
Christ himself. Also, it is not easy verbalisms about the Gospel,
but the Spirit of Christ incarnate in a man which is the deepest
and most effective form of communication of the Gospel today.
This level of communication is the core of pastoral care, and
should find expression through all of the activities of the pastor.

The principle of communication involved in our concept of
pastoral care is simply that the nature of any reality determines
the way in which it can be communicated. Mathematical reality
is such that it can be communicated through impersonal symbols.
On the other hand, the redemptive reality which is God's love is
deeply personal. It comes to each man in terms of his own existence and his own problems. It concerns each man's being as he is
related to Ultimate Being. A man suffers because of a broken
relationship in his personal existence. He finds healing through a
person who calls him back into a very personal unity of purpose
and meaning, who addresses him as a person, a Thou rather than
an It. A person may speak to us with his lips and reach only the
surface of our being, our conscious, intellectual processes. The
deeper level of being is reached by a person only through what
he is to us, and through our response of openness and trust to
him as a person. God in Christ makes Himself known to men in
the struggles of their being and becoming—Person to person,
Spirit to spirit. The pastor may proclaim the love of God verbally, but the reality of this love is not communicated unless the
pastor enters in love and understanding, in the power of the
Spirit of God, into the sufferings and estrangement of the individual person. Even in preaching to a large congregation, real
communication does not take place until something behind and
beyond the words of the preacher finds a positive response in the
very being of a hearer so that a process of growth or healing is
begun.

There is an incident in the life of Jesus which brings particular reinforcement to our interpretation. It is when Jesus is ac-
cused of casting out demons by the power of Beelzebub (Luke
11:14–23). After pointing out that a kingdom divided against
itself cannot stand, Jesus goes on to say, "But if it is by the finger
of God that I cast out demons, then the kingdom of God has
come upon you." In other words, the very process of healing a

man of a demon is in itself a proclamation of the Kingdom of God. In such healing something profound occurred between Jesus and the sick man, something which those about him could not observe. Only the results could be seen, but they could not be believed. The observers were frightened because the results bore witness to something beyond their understanding and they could not accept a deeper insight. Therefore it must be evil. But Jesus emphasized that the Kingdom of God became real in the very presence of himself with the possessed man, and in the healing that resulted.

Many pastors have a too limited and frightened view of their significance as pastors, and this seriously limits their effectiveness. They are more concerned with "not going too far" than they are in discovering the healing of self-giving, suffering love. In the very act of healing and of promoting growth, whether it be the healing of the fear of a little child, the guilt of an adolescent, or the sense of futility and meaninglessness in an adult, the Kingdom of God may be proclaimed and realized more surely than by most preachers from the pulpit. In the quality of loving relationships which meet the daily spiritual needs of persons so that growth becomes possible, the Kingdom is also proclaimed through demonstration. Pastoral care is not an adjunct to the ministry; it is the very core.

The early Church distinguished between two kinds of verbal communication, the kerygma and the didache. The first was the central proclamation of the Church, the work of God in Christ, particularly as revealed in the Cross and the Resurrection. The didache was the ethical teaching which followed upon the acceptance of the Gospel message. However, it is difficult to read the pages of the New Testament, particularly the Gospels, and not discover a third and deeper level of communication. The kerygma and didache formulate, structuralize, and elaborate in concepts the relationship which God offers men. But this living relationship in which deep reconciliation is experienced can never be known or communicated through verbal formulation alone. It was known to the first Christians through the Person of Jesus; when it is known in successive generations it is through persons who are able to manifest it on a nonverbal level. This is the difference between a theological statement on pastoral care

and pastoral care as a living relationship in which a healing love
is manifest. In the New Testament this is understood as the work
of the Holy Spirit, the Spirit of God in Christ, reaching out to
man's spirit. The pastor is called to continue the work of Christ
by loving men in a finite way and thus pointing to the redemptive love of God.

The concept of pastoral care as developed here moves beyond
any theology which is only proclaimed verbally. It returns to a
historical Jesus revealed in the Gospels, a Person authenticating
his words by his life, by what others experienced him to be. He
spoke with authority, not as one leaning on authorities. Of him
it was written: "We have beheld his glory, glory as of the only
Son from the father" (John 1:14). And again, "From his fullness
have we all received, grace upon grace" (John 1:16). Such interpretations of the Person of Jesus are grounded in the power and
grace which others felt in him as they were able to open their
lives to him in trust.

Modern theological scholarship offers some support at this
point. Paul Althaus[2] quotes Gunther Bornkamm's remark concerning Bultmann's position: "Jesus has become a mere fact of
salvation, and is no longer a person." Althaus goes on to say,
"The fact that the person of Jesus as such (of whose concrete
characteristics we can, in Bultmann's words, "now know practically nothing") has no place in the kerygma, leads to serious
theological consequences. The power of the Gospel to overcome
our unbelief depends on the fact that the kerygma includes the
gospels with their concrete picture of Jesus. In the picture of the
man Jesus we lay hold of the character of God, in the spiritual
countenance of Jesus we behold the countenance of God. The
living eyes of a man look at us out of the gospels and compel our
faith. The kerygma is a statement, a dogma, if we do not see it
filled out by the living picture of Jesus as the gospels portray
Him." And we are suggesting that in genuine pastoral care there
is an additional factor, a nonverbal expression of the meaning of
the Gospel through the relationship of pastor and person.

Pastoral experience, as well as the Gospel itself, clearly indicates the necessity of the mutual involvement of pastor and person. In this involvement the pastor is not just another person—a
father, a mother, a friend—but is one whose involvement demon-

strates and gives living substance to the message of God's grace. Effective pastoral care, that is, meeting a person at the point of his need, demands that the pastor become involved in the very existence and predicament of the person, his tensions, sufferings, meanings, values, joys. This involvement can take place only through a deeply empathic experience. The pastor cannot stand off and observe in detachment. He should not assume a relationship of control, manipulation, or domination toward others, nor should he permit them to exercise these attitudes over him. Pastoral involvement, sometimes called identification, requires that the pastor be his genuine self to others, and not put on a front. He seeks to understand how others feel by honestly admitting to himself how he would feel in a similar situation. He seeks to understand the needs, goals, and purposes of others, taking seriously their value system and the meaning they attach to experience. This identification is never complete—the pastor must always maintain a clear sense of his own identity as distinct from that of another.

Such involvement requires participation with others in their experience, rather than doing things for others or to them. It requires a genuine self-giving love, an inner freedom to do or be what is necessary to help another find his full self-realization. In such involvement the pastor is concerned to help others find their own answers, and he is very sensitive to understand and control any tendency in himself to become part of the answer. The pastor also identifies with the Gospel, with Christ in whose name he works, and with the Church, but these identifications should strengthen him to identify with those for whom Christ died.

This involvement, grounded in identification and empathy, is not possible by following directions. It depends upon the level of emotional maturity of the pastor. If he is emotionally immature, he will develop immature relationships with his people, without knowing what he is doing. Various characteristics of immaturity, such as dependence, passivity, and manipulation and control of others, will be manifest in the relationship of the emotionally immature pastor. More mature persons will sense such qualities and will avoid a deep relationship with him. The genuine pastor must maintain his own integrity at all times, otherwise he will be able to help no one.

Such empathic involvement is not easily accepted by all persons in our culture. Indeed, one source of problems is the inability of some persons to open themselves to another. Absolute trustworthiness is an essential quality in the helper. The pastor must be the kind of a person who can be so trusted that another will invite him to share the realities of his existence, especially those which are painful, in which he has already been hurt. Such trust and openness can come to the pastor, not because he has any particular brand of theology, but because he is a genuinely loving, trustworthy person. He also must have the wisdom to know what really helps and what does harm in various human situations. But the pastor should not expect that everyone will respond to him favorably.

The involvement of the pastor in the pastoral relationship is not just as another person, although the personal dimension of the life of the pastor is never eliminated, but is primarily as a servant of God, bringing a ministry of redemptive love. While many professions "do something" for others, the task of the pastor is not so much in the realm of doing as of being. It is a matter of being the kind of person who helps others find their own true relationship to God, is that inwardly they may become whatever in the grace of God they can become, and at the same time function adequately in relation to themselves and to their fellow men.

Communication on this level has the quality of revelation. It is always a two-way process; there can be no understanding of others unless we are able to reveal ourselves. In pastoral relationships, persons generally wait for the pastor to reveal himself, and their self-revelation is governed by the quality of what he reveals about himself. Any response to another person is a form of self-revelation; to respond is to reveal something about ourselves. It may reveal our defensiveness or our openness, our fear or our courage, or any other personal quality. God becomes known to man through his own self-revelation.

We constantly see in the counseling experience that for a person to reveal himself to another is also to make a self-discovery. Indeed, an essential element in the therapeutic process is that of helping persons find "insight," that is, self-discovery, by actually experiencing themselves in the presence of someone who knows how to accept and understand their revelation. Such communication is not primarily a matter of words, although words are involved. But deeper feelings and strivings must be revealed. The Christian doctrine of revelation has profound implications for pastoral care if we see revelation as a process that is continually deepening our relationships, by which we become known to each other and to ourselves in a mutual relationship before God. Many of us cannot understand and accept the revelation of God because our discovery and revelation of ourselves has been blocked.

The futility of communication in which there is no deep involvement, no revelation and self-discovery, is illustrated by the following editorial from the *Chicago Daily News,* January 27, 1964:

NO PLACE FOR JERRY HOLLINS

Ours is a big, rich, exciting city; its shops are bulging with goods, its streets full of shiny cars; its theaters and restaurants full of well-to-do people.

And there is Jerry Hollins.

Jerry Hollins was born in Louisiana, and lived there for 25 years.

But there is not much future for a young man in Louisiana if he is a Negro; and the word keeps coming down about how good things are up North, especially in Chicago.

Two years ago Jerry Hollins came to Chicago to look for work. He didn't find much, and when he found it, it didn't last long.

Recently he took to hanging around the Greyhound bus station, and when a policeman asked him why he was loitering there, and he didn't have a good reason, he was arrested for disorderly conduct.

The judge set his fine at $100. Hollins didn't have $100. He didn't have anything.

In the House of Correction he worked out the fine in the laundry. Nobody came to see him, and he listed no relatives.

At 9 a.m. Thursday he was let out of the House of Correction, and at 1:30 p.m. he crawled out on a ledge in the U.S. Court House rotunda, seven stories above the lobby floor.

It took him so long to work up his nerve that firemen were able to get there with a net, and when he jumped, they caught him and broke his fall. He suffered a broken pelvis, a collapsed lung, broken ribs, and other serious injuries.

Just before Hollins jumped a minister caught his attention. "God loves you," the minister said.

Hollins asked, "What God?"

Nobody seems to have given Jerry Hollins an answer.

This points to what is wrong with so much pastoral care—it stands back at a safe distance and verbalizes a message. There is no involvement with persons, no revelation and self-discovery, and no discovery of God. "What God?" is a question which can only be answered in a relationship in which revelation and discovery are simultaneous experiences.

The kind of involvement of which we have been speaking is characteristic of the relationship which Jesus had with those he met. In the words of James D. Smart,[3]

> Jesus' pastoral relationship with his disciples and with others was one in which he laid himself open to them in an unconditional way, interpenetrated their situation with his love and understanding, and took upon himself the burden of their sins, distresses, and anxieties. He gave himself to them, not in any sentimental way, but in the profoundest identification of himself with them. He made himself one with them, so that they were conscious of his not judging them from without but understanding them from within.

This view of pastoral care seems to be in conflict with certain theological views, particularly the doctrine of the "sovereignty of grace." Before we examine this doctrine specifically, a few words are necessary in regard to the relation of doctrine in general to human experience.

The pastor deals primarily with persons, not with ideas or doctrines. In this way he may differ radically from many theologians who are absorbed in ideas and are only theoretically concerned with persons—although we must recognize that this is not true of all theologians. However, the pastor needs to avoid the temptation of finding security in ideas to such an extent that he puts himself in something of an intellectual and operational strait jacket. When this occurs he will seek to put others in the same doctrinal framework.

The weakness of an approach which is primarily doctrinal is that the dynamic processes of human life cannot be controlled and manipulated or placed in a strait jacket without hurting persons. There is an element of spontaneity in human experience, and a drive toward autonomy and self-determination which is either crushed by a too rigid doctrinal approach or which may motivate a person to rebel and reject the whole of the Christian faith. On the other hand, it has been frequently remarked that people may seek the security of doctrine in order to avoid the heavy responsibility of autonomy. There are indications that this has taken place in recent years in the field of pastoral care and counseling.

An intellectual system can begin with a certain premise, and from there be developed by rejecting all contradictory ideas. But life itself cannot be confined to any system, since it is dynamic, always in motion, opening from within, or else deteriorating. Persons are not machines, and are not completely predictable in any logical or mathematical manner. Intellectual formulations may serve the purposes of life, but life should not be asked to serve the purposes of the formulations, that is, to stay within them. No finite mind has yet produced the infallible and completely comprehensive intellectual system. Systems therefore must be kept flexible—growing and changing with each new insight from life. This is particularly true for the pastor, who is dealing with the profound level of the life of the spirit which least of all is subject to man-made systems of operation. Perhaps this accounts for the fact that the work of the Holy Spirit has been so neglected—the Holy Spirit cannot be restricted to man's intellectual formulations.

The doctrine of the sovereignty and sufficiency of grace, coming down from the Reformers, is a good example of a religious insight which can be used either in a creative or a restrictive way. An illustration of its restrictive use is cited by George Hendry in discussing the Reformers. He says, "The sufficiency of grace alone left no need of correlation with anything on the part of man, but implied rather his total incapacity. . . . The Reformers rapidly lost interest in the human spirit altogether and for an obvious reason: When the full force of their new apprehension of the Gospel was deployed theologically, it seemed to obliterate the spirit of man and reduce him to the level of an inanimate object like a stone or tree."[4] Or in the words of Calvin, "Man is so enslaved by sin as to be of his own nature incapable of an effort, or even an aspiration, toward that which is good."[5]

Hendry presents philosophical, Biblical, and theological objections to this view of the sovereignty and sufficiency of grace, and we shall not summarize these here. We are more concerned at the moment to distinguish between two aspects of the problem particularly relevant to the pastor. The pastor, from the perspective of his Christian commitment, understands the ultimate nature of God and the finite nature of man. God in His ultimate nature is in no way dependent upon man. But God, as He manifests Himself to man, has made Himself dependent on man's response, or else man is an automaton, a puppet, and not a free spirit. That man has no power within himself to do some things for himself is belied by many creative experiences in pastoral care, even with those who are in a state of profound mental illness. That man does this in relationship, not by himself, is also indisputably evidenced in pastoral care. That a person has the ability to learn to control his own response to what is given him on a human level cannot be doubted. That he has the power to determine his response to God is unquestionable. God, in His gracious approach to man, does not take over and force him to make a favorable response.

One of the essentials of the pastor is a working understanding of the role of creation in human life. To assume that man's freedom and ability to arrive at decisions involving his own destiny are of his own making is false. Man is what he is in part through certain gifts and graces bestowed upon him in the act of creation. If man has freedom, it was given to him as a gracious act of God, the Creator. Man does not create his own freedom, but he participates actively in its realization. This is at least part of the meaning of the insight that man was made in the image of God. The gracious redemptive activity of God in Jesus Christ is directed toward the man whom God has already created. But redemption is not forced on man; man's co-operation is essential. Creation and redemption are thus two sides of the same coin; the power which man has to do something for himself is not of his own making but is a gift of God's creation. And it never comes to its fruition in isolation, but always in relationship to others. This is the essential truth in the idea of the sufficiency of grace. Grace is given in relationships.

John Wesley's concept of prevenient grace lies closer to the heart of pastoral experience. He says,[6]

There is no man that is in a state of mere nature; there is no man, unless he has quenched the Spirit, that is wholly void of the grace of God. No man living is entirely destitute of what is vulgarly called *natural conscience.* But this is not natural; it is more properly termed, *preventing grace.* Every man has a greater or less measure of this, which waiteth not for the call of man. Every man has, sooner or later, good desires, although the generality of men stifle them before they can strike deep roots, or produce any considerable fruit. . . . So that no man sins because he has not grace, but because he does not use the grace which he hath.

In pastoral care it is not enough to tell people that grace is available for them, but rather one must be to them a person through whom a measure of grace—often in terms of strength, courage, and hope—is experienced. When a counselor considers the amount of strength available within a troubled person, he is thinking in terms of prevenient grace, whether he uses these words or not.

The heart of our problem lies in the nature of man. Man lives and moves and has his being in an ultimate Creator-Redeemer God. God's redemptive process continues man's creation and perfects it. But human existence is on a finite level, and man has had difficulty in handling the tensions that arise out of the conflict between the demands and meanings of an ultimate, final relationship, and the more immediate, finite aspects of his nature and his existence. Scholars have formulated this problem in various ways. Tillich's[7] formulation of the problem of salvation in terms of existentialism is well known. Thornton,[8] following Bonhoeffer, uses the terms "ultimate" and "penultimate" in wrestling with the problem. Whatever terms the pastor uses to formulate the problem and the answers, he needs to understand the operational dynamics involved in persons. By this we mean that experiences on the proximate level of life, particularly in human relationships, are a determining factor in the individual's perception of, and response to, God and Christ. Much rebellion against God is really rebellion against human parents. The helpful pastor will seek to assist such persons to gain insight into, and work through, the destructive feelings developed on the human level as a means of resolving problems in their relationship or response to God. For this reason, verbal formulation is not sufficient, although when skillfully used it may prove helpful. Verbal formulation of religious meaning does not change the dynamic factors in an individual's perception and response. Many persons are so absorbed with the problems and difficulties on the proximate, existential level of life, and their powers of response are so dulled by both external and inner pressures, that they are unable to be concerned with ultimate meanings. To condemn them as sinners, or even to describe them in such terms, may mean that the pastoral concern is without redemptive purpose. The pastor must be concerned to alleviate the conditions, external and internal, which underlie their spiritual lethargy.

One illustration will suffice. Recently a student came to an interview after a class period in which Christian love had been discussed. One point stressed by the teacher was that Christian love involves the sharing of oneself with others. The student felt drawn to the idea and could see its applicability in his own life. Sharing himself with others was just what he could not do. He had built a shell around himself, and he found it very difficult to open himself to others. He had recently opened himself to another student in what seemed to be a friendship, but which developed quickly in dimensions which created intense guilt and frustration. So he had withdrawn again, and was more afraid than ever to open himself to anyone. The result of the class was an intense sense of guilt and frustration. He had received a verbal communication which he could see was directly related to his own experience. The communication did not create the problem, but merely put it into words and intensified his awareness. But his thinking led to dead ends: the problem remained, "How do I get to the point where I can overcome my fear and open myself to others?" He could talk about the problem in its Christian theological dimensions, but this only brought on a deeper level of anxiety as he saw himself unable to be what he thought God wanted him to be. The confrontation with himself in terms of basic attitudes was very deep. In terms of understanding the roots of those attitudes and of working them out so that they no longer controlled him, nothing had yet been accomplished. The accomplishment of this was a real work of pastoral care, requiring a long relationship with a person of genuine love, understanding, and skill to help him overcome his fear and respond in trust. He had to have help with problems on the human level primarily within himself before the ultimate relationships could be resolved. The meaning of God's love for him had to be mediated through a person in order for it to become his own experience; this could not be made to happen by verbalization alone.

The idea of the sovereignty and sufficiency of grace must be balanced, as it is in the New Testament and in life, by man's freedom and responsibility on the level of the proximate, the human aspects of life. That man has no power to control or manipulate God should be obvious. That God has not made man to be an automaton, a puppet, seems evident. A person's response to the grace of God is controlled within him. Man is always in tension because there is a power working within him that is not of his own making, yet as far as his individual existence is concerned, he has freedom and responsibility of decision. He must also experience the consequences of his decision within himself.

And there is another source of man's tension. His freedom and autonomy is threatened by the fact that there is much in man's existence which determines the manner in which his freedom is used. The drive toward autonomy begins to express itself early in life, but it may be thwarted and denied by anxious parents. Relationships with humans may be such that an individual gradually loses his power of autonomy as he matures. This means that he will become sick, that is, unable to function as a human being. If his sickness is extreme, he is relieved from all human responsibility and decisions are made for him. Recovery or cure may require a long relationship with a genuinely loving and understanding person.[9] But the avoidance of such a tragedy in the first place also requires a relationship of love and understanding within a framework of constructive values in the entire process of growing up.

Truly creative pastoral care takes into account the various dimensions of human life and gives them adequate consideration. A one-sided emphasis on either the experience of grace or that of freedom or on the determining influences in human life leads to a distorted approach. Theological ideas such as the complete impotence of man may express the power of guilt to produce self-depreciation. On the other hand, an overemphasis on man's powers to save himself apart from a living relationship with God may express man's pride and defensiveness. The pastor will need to understand theological ideas not only according to their theological meaning, but also in terms of the way in which they are used defensively by persons.

The question of God's power to work directly in human life is usually raised at this point. That God has the power to do this is not in question. The question is whether God does enter human life and take over against man's will. Are there times when God rescinds a man's freedom and forces him into some particular behavior? Or are all of God's relationships with man characterized by grace which permits a free response, even rejection?

The question of God's working directly in human life, that is, operating apart from man's freedom, needs examination from another angle. The pastor is likely to find some persons who are sure this has happened to them. Sometimes—not always—these folks are found in a mental hospital. They are the victims of a psychotic condition in which contents from their own unconscious is identified as the voice of action of God. There is much compulsiveness in such experience, that is, the individual does feel compelled to think or act in certain ways and may believe that God is forcing him to do this. In milder forms, this same experience may occur in almost any religious community. These experiences convey a deep sense of the mysterious and the pastor must not permit himself to be misled by this. While he should not openly dispute the person's interpretation, he must also avoid agreeing with that interpretation and thus confirming his illness.

That God does work in human life is a deep conviction of the Christian faith. There is a sense in which man's entire existence is created and sustained by the love and power of God. This is part of the meaning of the doctrine of Creation and of Wesley's concept of prevenient grace. But on the level of conscious awareness, God works through a gracious, loving relationship in which the co-operation of the human agent is an active component. Prayer and worship are experiences in which such conscious awareness and co-operation can develop on the part of man; or they may be used for the opposite result. God does work in human life, but in a way which does not rob man of the basic meaning of "personhood," the power of autonomous decision within the framework of responsibility.

Man, then, is a finite creature who has the capacity to experience meanings and relationships which are seen as being on the level of the ultimate. As a finite creature, he may know God, his creator. This is the crowning characteristic of personhood, the power to shape the immediate in terms of ultimate goals and purposes, to experience a personal relationship with God. God's revelation of Himself in Christ was communication in personal relationship. Insight into ultimate purposes, goals, and relationships must become operative on the levels of the immediate and the finite. Otherwise they will have no significance for the finite aspects of the life of man, a situation which has frequently existed in religion. It is only as these two aspects of the life of man become dynamically related that man finds his fulfillment.

Since pastoral care is primarily communication on the level of relationships, the incarnational principle must be operative in all of the pastor's relationships. Otherwise, he may speak the words of the faith without communicating the reality of the faith. This in no way limits the sovereignty and sufficiency of grace; it only describes the basis on which that grace becomes real. And unless that grace does become real in the immediate or proximate levels of life, unless it has something to bring to persons as they undergo the joys, conflicts, and suffering of life, religion becomes only a sick fantasy about the next world. We already have too much of this.

The principle of the incarnation not only involves the pastor, but the entire Christian community. From the earliest days of the Hebrew-Christian faith, God chose to work through the faithful community. The fact that this community was not always faithful did not destroy the purposes of God, but it did interfere with their fruition. Where a living Church is brought into existence, there God works in and through the human community. Some churches are so dead spiritually that it is no wonder that persons brought up in them do not understand this truth. They cannot understand what they have not experienced.

On the level of spirit the only method of communication of reality is through experience. All men need a priest, and all who would grow into the Christian faith need a community in which grace is manifest—not because of God's inadequacy, but because of men's inability to comprehend what they have not experienced. Some of the importance of the doctrine of the priesthood of all believers lies in the fact that before a man can honestly open himself to God, he may first need to learn to open himself to one who stands in the place of God. A person who has not known love on the human level cannot comprehend the meaning of the love of God. He will respond to the verbal message of the love of God in terms of infantile fantasy grounded in deprivation, a fantasy of infantile magic, and his religious experience will be highly emotional with no deep volitional content. Or he will reject the idea of God's love because he is unable to experience any sense of inner reality in it. Or he may struggle to accept the idea of God's love without any deep sense of reality or meaning. Love becomes real only through loving relationships, not through words about love.

It may be objected that this interpretation will encourage the pastor to "play God." This brings up one of the professional hazards of the ministry. Such problems grow from two sources. One is the sense of inferiority in the pastor against which he reacts with ideas of being a superior person. The other is the very responsibility which the pastor fulfills as a preacher and priest. This places him in the position of one who is standing in the place of God and speaking for God. The great professional temptation of the pastor is to gradually and unconsciously proceed from his role as a representative of God to an unconscious fantasy of himself as God. Then he begins to play God: to become authoritarian, dictatorial, dogmatic, punishing; to assert the superiority of his wisdom and theology; and to seek to overpower others with his position. We do not mean that these are the characteristics of God as he is seen in Christ. Certainly they are not. They are the characteristics which the human ego takes on when it tries to play God.

Understanding the meaning of his relationship to others and to God should help the pastor avoid the temptation to "play God." For when he sees himself as something of a mediator, that is, one whose relationship may have meaning to others on two levels, the proximate and the ultimate, the human and the divine, he should be moved to humility. Indeed, if we understand Paul's interpretation of the incarnational experience correctly, it involves emptying oneself of pride. "Though he was in the form of God, [Jesus] did not count equality with God a thing to be grasped, but emptied himself, taking the form of a servant, being born in the likeness of men" (Phil. 2:1-11). It may be objected that this statement applies to Jesus but not to the rest of us, and in a special way this is true. But in another sense this intepretation is not limited to Jesus. The pastor must likewise "empty himself" and take on the "form of a servant," accepting his human existence as one through which God can work for His own glory and for the reconciliation of man to Himself. God is not an authoritarian director or a supermanipulator of man's will, but One who reveals Himself by sharing human suffering in self-giving love on the Cross. His ministers, if they are to bring to men the reality of this love, have no other way but through self-giving love in which human pride in intellect or power are transformed into suffering love. The genuine pastoral relationship is an experience in humility.

The pastor, then, is one through whom the love of God is made real in human relationships in which the pastor's love speaks of the greater love of God. In suggesting that the pastor is something of a mediator, we are well aware that the New Testament speaks of the "one mediator between God and man, the man Christ Jesus" (I Tim. 2:5). Accepting the uniqueness of the mediatory work of Christ, we must go on to emphasize again that Jesus himself indicated to his disciples that they were to carry on his work in his Spirit, and through power which would be given to them as they needed. As Luther put it, our task is to be as "little Christs to our neighbors."[10] Or as a modern theologian puts it, "Because the grace of God portrayed itself perfectly in Christ, it can portray itself imperfectly in others."[11] It is indeed a miracle that God's grace can enter human experience through the imperfect love of another human being and still make itself known in its fullness. Such mediation is grounded in the divine initiative through creation and redemption; it promotes rather than interferes with communion with God; it places the pastor in a living relationship with God and man, that is, he is to love those whom he serves just as God in Christ has loved both him and them. We would not confine this level of communication to the pastor. It is also the responsibility of the layman. But we are saying that it is this dimension which distinguishes real pastoral care from mere pastoral activity. The pastor should have a level of training and wisdom in such matters beyond that which most laymen are not privileged to acquire.

Pastoral Care and the Holy Spirit

In stressing the place of relationships in the communication of the Gospel, and the incarnational nature of genuine Christian relationships, we are obviously approaching what has been called the extension of the Incarnation. Christian thought has largely rejected this concept, probably in order to preserve the uniqueness of the Person of Christ. While this may be structurally and theologically sound, the pastor, constantly dealing with the processes of life rather than with formulations about them, must keep his attention focused on what happens between persons and within persons in Christian experience. In Christian thought this means moving away from the concept of the extension of the Incarnation to that of the Holy Spirit. In the New Testament the Holy Spirit is the gift of Christ to his disciples, it is the presence of Christ within the experience of his followers and "where two or three are gathered together." We therefore turn to a consideration of the relation of pastoral care to the work of the Holy Spirit.

There is a fundamental problem as to the meaning of human spirit and Holy Spirit, and of their relationship. It is not our intention to enter into this at any length.[12] However, pastoral care cannot accept a theological point of view which depreciates the human spirit or person. The pastor has many opportunities to observe the tremendous potential of the human spirit for growth and healing even under the most adverse conditions. We shall not attempt to draw a line between the activity of the human spirit and the Holy Spirit, for the Holy Spirit is manifest to man through a quality of relationship which makes such lines highly artificial and misleading. But the human spirit is completely passive only in those persons suffering from deeply, neurotic passive dependence, and even here the potential for activity is present. To make such pathological conditions normative for the Christian faith is a mistake. The view that depreciates and devalues the human spirit is as deadly to creative pastoral care as is exclusive adherence to modern psychological determinism. Indeed, such adherence may represent refusal to accept the truly creative, spontaneous, and responsible aspects of the human spirit.

The concept of spirit needs to be taken out of the area of magic, ghosts, and goblins, and neither should it be used to explain in a vague way what we do not understand or to excuse ourselves from some kind of responsibility. Arnold B. Come in his *Human Spirit and Holy Spirit*,[13] and following Kierkegaard, asserts that "man *qua* man . . . is a realized indissolvable unity of body and soul, denoted by the term 'spirit,' or in contemporary language, 'self' or 'person.' Again he speaks of the 'I,' the self, the person, the spirit." This places the manifestation of spirit exactly within the framework of personal relationships: man as spirit or self is called into being in relationship with other selves, and ultimately in relationship with God, the Supreme Self. God communicates to man through the manifestation of His Spirit, through His presence as a living Person in relationship with finite persons. In pastoral care, the spirit or self of the pastor, his presence or relationship with another person or persons, is a context through which the Holy Spirit may manifest itself.

The human spirit or self is weak when it experiences isolation or estrangement. Its growth and well-being require a relationship in which grace, in the form of love, support, and nurturance of others, is received. Such a relationship can take place on the human level. Human relationships always contain ambiguous elements, and in the relationship of the pastor there is the possibility of doing harm as well as good. No other quality of relationship, however, can fulfill the conditions which make it possible for another to respond in trust—the kind of trust which is essential for the development of the potentiality for autonomy. Thus the person who trusts must take a "leap of faith" in that he is never sure on the human level when a gracious person will become a hurtful one. The pastor needs to become aware of the subtle ways in which he might hurt others. It is only the Holy Spirit that is free from such ambiguity and ambivalence.

But such experiences of grace are not for the selfish possession of the individual. The self which seeks to hold on to what he has been given will lose it. Grace is given that it may in turn be given again. It seems to be an unalterable law of life that as we have received, so do we give. The human spirit, or self, is enriched by gracious relationships with others, impoverished and deprived—and as a result distorted—by relationships without meaning. In turn, the human spirit gives as it has received. As we have been loved, so we learn to love; as we have been accepted in grace, so are we able to accept others in grace. We give out of abundance of spirit, not out of poverty of spirit.

Dillistone[14] describes the results of the activity of the Holy Spirit as life in unity, the gift of power, the establishment of order and insight into the meaning and glory of God as seen in Jesus Christ. The importance of these activities for pastoral care should be obvious. But it should also be evident that each of them is manifest in personal relationships. They are the manifestation of the presence of God with persons. In a partial sense they may be the result of the presence, or association, of one human being with another, depending on the nature of that association. Two words have been used in recent years to describe God's relation to man, and also to interepret the pastor's relation to others. They are both military words: "encounter" and "confrontation." They grow out of experiences of armed conflict, where one side aggressively overcomes the other. The use of these warlike terms has evidently fulfilled a deep psychological need in many of our contemporaries. However, the Biblical word for God's being with man is the one we have already used: "presence." It is a gracious presence, but for this very reason it may be disturbing and guilt-producing, calling men to responsibility and leading to decision. One has often heard young ministers talk about confronting others, and inevitably such talk is hostile and aggressive. These are hardly the means through which the Gospel or the human aspects of the life of the spirit can be made real to others.

Rather, the communication of the Gospel in pastoral care becomes effective through what Paul describes as the "fruits of the Spirit." He enumerates these as love, joy, peace, patience, kindness, goodness, faithfulness, gentleness, and self-control qualities one might ascribe to the personality of Christ. When a person of these qualities associates with another in a significant relationship, something creative and redemptive may occur. But these qualities spring from the deep, interior levels of personality, within the self, or the spirit. They are called into being through a relationship in which they are manifested by the pastor, and they evoke from the recipient similar responses. They are qualities of the true human self in its fullest development. They are also the human side of God in Christ, that is, the qualities inspired by the Spirit of God in human life. They are the fruits of the Spirit and represent the deepest motivation of which a human being is capable. The pastor, in his relationships with others, will communicate these qualities in so far as he possesses them. They are not given once for all, but are constantly recreated, in part through communion with God and in part through human relationships.

There is another aspect of the work of the Holy Spirit in the communication of the Gospel. The mediation of the fruits of the Spirit in human relationships strikes deep in the mind and spirit of the recipient. To feel oneself genuinely loved, accepted, and addressed as a person strikes deep chords of response. It may, under some conditions, such as in the men possessed by demons, (Matt. 8:28-29), bring a response of intense fear and rejection. we have seen persons who, because of deep emotional and spiritual injuries, seemed completely incapable of making anything but a negative response to love or understanding. On the other hand, we have seen the opposite: the individual with a strong sense of having been rejected and unloved reaching out eagerly to grasp even a weak expression of love. The great helpers of mankind have been those who have been able to speak, sometimes in utter silence, to the deeper, creative levels of other persons.

It has been said that in psychotherapy the unconscious of the therapist speaks directly to the unconscious of the patient. In the words of a therapist,[15] "the unconscious of the psychotherapist must move toward the unconscious longing of the patient and must promise the latter the fulfillment of that longing."

This process is at work in pastoral care, even though it may not be recognized. It may be functioning between the preacher and some of the people in the pews, as well as in other pastoral relationships. It should be also recognized that in using such verbal symbols as God, Father, Christ, love, forgiveness, and in effectively communicating some of the spiritual reality for which these words stand, the pastor may be speaking more directly and effectively to the unconscious than does the therapist. Certainly much conscious meaning may be communicated through religious forms, and also the unconscious attitudes of the pastor are communicated without words. Putting this in theological terminology, we can say that spirit truly speaks to spirit, both through and without the use of words.

We turn now to one of Paul's (I Cor. 2:10-13) interpretations of the work of the Spirit:

> For the Spirit searches everything, even the depths of God. For what person knows a man's thoughts except the spirit of the man which is in him? So also no one comprehends the thoughts of God except the Spirit of God. Now we have received not the spirit of the world, but the Spirit which is from God, that we might understand the gifts bestowed on us by God. And we impart this in words not taught by human wisdom but taught by the Spirit, interpreting spiritual truths to those who possess the Spirit.

We will try to understand this passage in the light of what we have been saying about verbal and nonverbal communication. The spirit of a man does know what is in that man, and it knows what it is seeking from others. The conscious self, however, in its weakness, may be seeking to conceal rather than to discover the truth about himself. But even in this condition the man's own spirit may be restless, not wanting to face the pain of knowing but still searching for the answer to his suffering. The drive toward cure may be operating even in persons with deep psychotic conditions. The spirit of a man does search the deepest thought, feelings, and motives of the man. And the Spirit of God does search everything, the depths of man and the depths of God. When the Christian pastor meets his people with some measure of the fruits of the Spirit, something creative may happen on a level deeper than consciousness. The Spirit of God, through the spirit of the pastor, may speak to a deep unconscious need and start a process of growth which eventually culminates in redemption. But this culmination must include the conscious self: that which was hidden must be brought to light and either accepted into the self or consciously modified or given up. A truly redemptive Christian experience requires conscious, responsible understanding and decisions. An experience in which the conscious self comes under the domination and control of unconscious impulses or feelings needs to be carefully scrutinized and worked through. But even then there are levels of human experience which are in the realm of mystery, and can be only dimly apprehended, as through a glass darkly. One suspects that this passage from Paul contains part of his reflections on his own inner turmoil before and after the Damascus road experience, and that he is not able to express fully all that he feels or all that has happened to him, but that he is struggling to interpret it. One seems justified in suspecting that on the occasion of the stoning of Stephen (Acts 7:54-8:3), some powerful unconscious communication took place, and that the Spirit spoke through Stephen to a young man named Saul. The modern pastor needs to be as much a religious psychologist of the unconscious and a theologian of the Spirit as was Paul.

The Holy Spirit is the presence of Christ in human life. It is an experience that can be partly understood, yet it is also clothed in mystery. But its results may be seen in human life, in the fruits of the spirit. The best analogy for understanding the personal relationship of God with man is the personal relationship of man to man. A relationship between persons, or selves, on the human level, is the source of much of man's glory and meaning—or of his destructiveness. But human relationships condition and predispose man to perceive and respond to the presence of Christ in like terms. Thus the demoniac (Matt. 8:28-29), possessed by an evil spirit, or self, begged Christ to depart from him. The pastor cannot manipulate or control the Holy Spirit. But his presence with a person, the quality of his spirit, may remove or create human obstacles to the work of the Holy Spirit. The pastor needs to study his relationships, how he responds to others and how others respond to him. This area is to some extent within his own autonomous control and power to change.

In this chapter we have introduced the concept of pastoral care as the communication of the Gospel to persons at the point of their need. We have stressed the inner reality of the relationship of God to man, and have asked how this is communicated. Verbal formulations communicate about this relationship. The reality of the relationship can be communicated only through experience. This has led to an incarnational theory of communication, and consequently of the work of the pastor. Or in terms of more traditional theology, it is the work of the Spirit, of the Holy Spirit present with man's spirit, bringing man's spirit, or self, to

its fulfillment. For testimony of the incarnational aspect of communication of the Gospel we go to a scholar in the field of
missions, Eugene A. Nida, who in his book *Message and Mission*[16] says,

All divine communication is essentially incarnational, for it comes only
in words, but in life. Even if a truth is given only in words, it has no
real validity until it has been translated into life. Only then does the
Word of life become life to the receptor. The words are in a sense
nothing in and of themselves. . . . In the Incarnation of God in Jesus
Christ, the Word (the expression and revelation of the wisdom of
God) became flesh. This same fundamental principle has been followed
throughout the history of the church, for God has constantly chosen
to use not only words but human beings as well to witness to His grace;
not only the message, but the messenger; not only the Bible, but the
Church.

❧ 3 ❧
The Gospel for Persons
Who Is a Person?

THE concept of pastoral care that we have been developing is not analogous to a circle which has a center; it is more like an ellipse, which has two foci. One focus is, of course, the Gospel; the other is the person for whom the Gospel is meant. In any ellipse there is always a dynamic tension between the two foci. In pastoral care the tension exists between the Gospel and the person. Omit either of these foci, and pastoral care quickly becomes something else. This means that the pastor must not only know and know about the Gospel; he must also know and know about persons.

If we take a Biblical approach to persons, we soon meet the question which was stated by the author of the eighth Psalm, "What is man that thou art mindful of him." What is man? Christian theology has sought an answer to this question, and we need not elaborate its answer here. Man is made in the image of God, man is a fallen sinner, man stands in need of the salvation which is from God in Christ. In these elements all men share and share alike. Individual experience is an expression of a universal truth.

But even as the Psalmist asks his question, he shifts his point of view, "That thou art mindful of him, . . . and that thou dost care for him." This is a shift from an impersonal "what" to a personal "who." He shifts from man in the mass to the individual. His question now becomes "Who is this person?" For when a relationship of caring is introduced, man ceases to be identified as one of a mass, and he stands out as a person. God as an I always addresses man as a thou, not as an it or a thing. It is this personal relationship which calls an individual into being as a person.[1]

The experience of God's meeting an individual as a person is amply illustrated in the Bible. The revelation of Isaiah (Chapter six) in the temple was an experience of the presence of God. A gracious presence summoned Isaiah into greater being as a person by calling him into a relationship which involved a mission. The question here was not "what will go for us?" but "who will go for us?"

When a man becomes aware of the presence of God he also becomes aware of himself as a person. This was the question Moses raised as he experienced the presence of God: "Who am I that I should go to Pharaoh?" (Exod. 3:1-15). And when God wanted to identify himself to Moses, he did not do so by means of a string of theological abstractions, but by identifying himself in personal relationship—he was the God of Abraham, Isaac, and Jacob. And throughout the pages of the Four Gospels we see Jesus meeting persons in terms of who they were, in personal relationships which reached toward individual need. He was constantly calling upon men to measure their relationship with themselves, with others, and with God against the quality of his personal relation to them. To him they were "who" or "thou," not things or an it.

It is my purpose to identify the pastoral approach with the "who" rather than with the "what." But let us first distinguish between them a little more clearly. When we ask, "What is man?" we are lumping all men together and asking about common traits. The answer is then to be found in generalizations in which the individual person is lost. "All men are sinners" is just such a generalization. It may be true enough, but the meaning of the actual personal experience of sin is lost. Such an approach makes the individual one of a class, and it thus reduces him from a person to a thing. It leads to concepts of a deterministic nature, whether answered in theological or psychological terms. It robs the individual of his uniqueness and distracts him from the personal quality of his existence. A generalization of this kind has certain values, but it is completely inadequate as a basis for the communication of the Gospel, for the Gospel concerns a living relationship and is communicated in its deeper levels through relationship.

When we ask the "who" question we move from the general to

the particular, from mankind to a man, a person, a unique, experiencing being of dignity and worth. The "who" question can never be answered in the abstract, but only in a personal relation. "Who do you say that I am?" asked Christ, not what (Matt. 16:13-15). To answer this question his disciples had to enter into a personal relationship with him, through which they also discovered something of who they were. No man can tell you who you are, but each man you meet demands something of you which, in turn, to some extent creates who you are. Thus the relationship between a mother and a child brings to each of them a new self, a new being. Likewise the relationship between friends, between husband and wife, between pastor and person, between man and God. "If any one is in Christ he is a new creation" (II Cor. 5:17). In such a relationship the individual experiences himself as an autonomous person called upon to choose, and in his choices and decisions he becomes something he has not already been.

When we ponder the meaning of who we are as distinct from what we are, we may discover that concentrating on the "what" question is really an escape from responsibility. For we can describe ourselves and others in endless abstractions without coming anywhere near our own experience. Or we can talk endlessly on an intellectual level about the meaning of life without ever facing the personal meaning of our own existence. To see ourselves as one of a class removes the anxiety which accompanies the sense of personal uniqueness or individuality. The tendency to conformity in our culture has been commented upon frequently. It is one thing to describe oneself as a sinner like all other men. It is quite another thing to become aware of the actual experience of sin in our own life, to come to ourselves as the Prodigal came to himself and face the decision that such awareness demands. All of us would like to be lost in the crowd, but salvation comes only in becoming what God in his wisdom intended us to become as individual persons. We meet the God who is in Christ only in personal relationship, and in this meeting we become new persons. But we can become so engrossed in the intellectual concepts and generalizations of the faith, in the answers to the "what" questions, that we successfully avoid the deeper responsibilities of "who?"

Man as Spirit

In speaking of the "what" and "who" of persons, we are dealing with a Biblical insight into the nature of man; his aspect as creature on the one hand, and as spirit on the other. The Biblical account of creation links man solidly with biological creation. Man's physical body was created first; then God "breathed into his nostrils the breath of life; and man became a living being" (Gen.2:7). Man shares the physical and organismic levels of life with other living creatures. As such he is subject to the processes of birth and death, to suffering and pain, and to many other contingencies of existence. But man is distinctive because he knows an existence on another level—as a living soul, made, according to the Genesis account, "in the image of God." Here the "soul" expresses the ultimate dimension in man's nature, which would include not only man's capacity for self-awareness and self-transcendence but also his capacity for awareness of the presence of God, and of meaning on a level beyond that of his earthly existence. With this there is also a unique capacity for a level of autonomy. Man has the degree of freedom to accept or reject demands, relationships, or meanings perceived as being the will of God.

But man is not a dualism; he is a unity. And the unity or synthesis of body and soul has been called "spirit." For what is "breathed into man," that is, what is given to him in relationships, comes through the bodily as well as through the "soulish" dimensions of his being. And how he receives, assimilates, and gives unique expression to grace in his relationships, is accomplished through the physical as well as through the "soulish" dimensions of his being. From a Christian point of view, to the usual levels of psychosomatic unity (chemical, physical, mental, social, environmental) must be added "spirit," the spirit of man, as the crowning level. The spirit of man is the synthesis of unity (or failure of unity) of a man's total being in relation to himself, to others and to God expressed in terms of meaning, value, and obligation. It is the spirit of a man of which we are really speaking when we ask, Who is he? A man's identity is the synthesis, or dynamic organization, of his total being as it has emerged through his human and divine relationships. A man's identity is also the expression of his spirit.

By spirit then we mean the self, or person, in the dynamic synthesis and meaning which an individual possesses within himself and in his relationship with others.[2] Whatever transcendent qualities we understand as belonging to the self, or spirit, we must see as undeveloped potentials that achieve healthy growth or distortion in the crucible of human relationships beginning at birth. This is the corrective that empirical psychology applies to a religious concept of self which sees the self divorced from the total processes of becoming. The self is the expression of the organic unity of the individual, not a separate entity. What happens on the physical level of the life of an individual then affects his self, or spirit, just as what happens to him as a whole person will affect his physiological functioning. The problem as to how a part of the individual gains control of the whole person, as in illness, and how the self, or spirit, may regain control and reorganize the functions of the parts of an individual, is elucidated by our understanding of the processes of illness on the one hand, and the processes of therapy or cure on the other.

This brings us to a statement of the central need of a person, or self, a question which is at the core of our concept of pastoral care. We can state this very simply. It is the need for a person to become himself, to fulfill the image of God within him, to give actuality to the potential for which he was created. But such fulfillment cannot be described in any final or static terms, since we are dealing with constantly moving and changing life processes. It must be formulated in terms of living relationships—the individual in relation to God, in relation to other persons, and in relation to himself. This means formulation in terms of being rather than of doing, in terms of Paul's "fruits of the Spirit" rather than in terms of acts or behavior.

The concept of the needs of persons in pastoral care must also take into account what is understood today as empirical needs, that is, those needs learned in experience. Psychologists have formulated a concept of learned needs. There has been some discussion of learned needs in contrast to basic or inborn needs. The psychologist, may ignore the ultimate dimension, and this is justifiable as long as we recognize that his point of view does not give a full account of the nature of man. Pastoral care should take into consideration the needs of persons which arise on the empirical level. However, an adequate theory of pastoral care cannot be based only on a formulation of learned needs, but must see man in his ultimate dimensions. An illustration of what we mean is the concept of the need for love. Some psychologists may formulate this need solely in terms of experience, without any reference to the nature of man. However, in the New Testament the need for love is firmly grounded in the nature of God and man, but it is also elaborated—experientially—in religious rather than in psychological terms. The psychologist may indicate that the need for love is learned through the love of the mother, but the New Testament adds another dimension; that is, we love because we are first loved by God.

The central need of persons has been thought of by theology as salvation. Man is a sinner standing in need of salvation. This concept has suffered a certain distortion—viewed from the perspective of persons—because sin has become defined as actions, not relationships that is, statically, not dynamically. Salvation has also been made a fixed experience, contingent upon accepting a given verbal formulation of the Christian faith, or undergoing a certain type of emotionally conditioned experience, or adhering to certain ritualistic forms. All these approaches are characterized by legalism in one form or another. But many persons who have found "salvation" through these approaches have not found fulfillment. They found no inner peace, no freedom from moralism, no release of their capacity to love, and very frequently the sense of forgiveness they experienced was a matter of repression of guilt feelings rather than release from such feelings in a new and creative relationship. The idea of salvation is a fulfillment of the self before itself, before other persons, and before God—or the actualization of something of the image of God—produces a kind of existential anxiety to which many respond by seeking refuge in static formulations which at least have the virtue of seeming concrete. But if pastoral care is to be concerned with the genuine cure of souls, it must see its function as that of helping persons to become what God in His creative wisdom intended them to become. This is not merely following a blueprint for human life, but living out a personal existence in a genuine relationship of trust and love.

Theology and Pastoral Care

This concept of pastoral care throws light on a problem which has come to the fore in recent years: the insistence by both pastors and theologians that theological concepts must be utilized more fully in pastoral care. Certain persons in the pastoral care movement have been criticized for being too psychologically oriented and not enough theologically so. Some authors have advanced the idea that pastoral care is really theological conversasation with an individual, whereas preaching is theological conversation with a group.[3] So far none of these books has really clarified the issues involved, except that pastoral care must become a form of theological indoctrination! But is it not yet clear that a person may be thoroughly indoctrinated in a given theological or moralistic position and still lose his own soul, and that indoctrination in itself may contribute heavily to the loss of the self?

Part of the problem here is a confusion of method. Theology is a method of interpreting Christian experience in intellectual terms. It states this interpretation in terms which are assumed to be universally valid. Thus it seeks to answer the "what" question. There is a real value in this as long as we understand the method and purpose of theological interpretation. But we must remember that the process moves in one direction, from experience to interpretation, and not from interpretation to experience. In this process of transformation, energy flows to the symbol, not from the symbol. The Christian faith is the experience of a relationship, including all of the processes involved in such a relationship. The fact that many persons have given intellectual assent to an interpretation, to a creed or a doctrine, or to an institution, in the belief that they have found salvation, only proves our point. For these persons have found only a kind of verbal or legal salvation; they have not found the freedom of the Gospel to become their real selves.

Intellectual assent to a doctrine without experiencing of the personal relationship implied in the doctrine is responsible for the split between theological beliefs and life processes which is often observed in persons. Intellectually, such persons believe that God loves them, but they do not experience this in personal relationships. Or they may accept the Christian faith creedally as it was preached to them, but their lives are controlled by fear. An example of this is to be found in the words of a pastor,[4] a man who felt ineffective and anxious in spite of fine intellectual abilities and personal talents. About himself he says,

There is no question about guilt feelings arising out of any sense of satisfaction I find in my work. This fight is in myself. It relates to my concept of the Christian life, of sin and salvation. I have no problem here philosophically nor theologically. I understand that the love of God does involve some self-regard. But my emotions do not fit in. I don't know why. The experience has not accompanied the concept. I have never experienced salvation as a life process. But philosophically I have not found any better system. But I have not gotten these together. I read Kierkegaard and find that he had the same problem. Underneath I am sure that this causes me real pain, but consciousness won't admit the pain to court.

When this man says that the experience has not accompanied the concept, he is speaking for us all. For experience never accompanies the concept unless there is at the same time a personal relationship which gives the concept reality in the deeper levels of our being.

The method of the theologian is that of interpretation, but the method of the genuine pastor is that of personal relationships, using interpretation to give intellectual substance to a reality which has been or is being experienced. And when the theologian becomes pastor, as sometimes he does, he moves from the level of concepts to the level of personal relations.

We have spoken of the necessity for the pastor to be involved in the experiences of persons. This means that he should not only preach about such things as sin, suffering, love, and forgiveness, but he must meet, in the pulpit and out of it, individuals in a personal relationship which makes it possible for them to become aware of, and talk about, "my sin," "my suffering," "my need for love and forgiveness," or "my need to be forgiving." In other words, he must know and understand the language of personal experience—what a person means when he says "I think," "I feel," "I am," "I hate," "I love," "I fear," "I ought." Also language is used to conceal personal experience and its meaning, and the pastor must learn to listen to this also and understand what it means. And he must learn to feel with the person, and to sense how he himself would respond if he were in a similar situation as well as how the other person is responding. The pastor's own perceptions of life and its meaning may not correspond to those of another person, but he must learn to deal with others in terms of their perceptions.

A large part of the personal relations which constitute pastoral care is the experience of communicating. The individual needs to be able to communicate or reveal himself to the pastor and find his revelation accepted and understood. Only then can the pastor's communication or conversation be guided by a genuine understanding of the Gospel as it relates to this particular individual's existence. Genuine pastoral care demands that we cease subjecting the individual to the various mass-production methods that we have developed in our churches and begin to deal with him in terms of his own individual experience in the light of the Gospel. We need to learn to understand the language by which persons, including ourselves, reveal themselves and also conceal themselves.

Dimensions of Persons

We turn now to certain dimensions of "personhood" which are important for pastoral care.

One dimension which the pastor must learn to respect is privacy. As a basic characteristic of persons, privacy is a function of individuality. To be an individual means to draw boundaries, or to seek boundaries where the self begins and ends. Psychoanalysts often speak of ego-boundaries. Here we are thinking of privacy as an essential dimension of persons in which the self learns to distinguish itself from what is not itself, and to form some relationship to each. One essential power of the self is the ability to exclude or to take in, to define its own being as distinct from, but in relation to, what is not self.

The dimension of privacy, under the stimulus of anxiety, often becomes elaborately defensive: a wall is built around the self and "no trespassing" signs erected to keep even ourselves out. The various defense mechanisms elaborated by psychoanalysis function to this end. Thus the basic dimension of privacy becomes distorted in ways which restrict or even destroy the growth of the self. Because we have been hurt, made to feel anxious, or deprived of satisfactions in our personal relationships, we respond defensively and want to keep others out. A sense of the disapproval of others, and even of a part of ourselves, causes us to keep some of our own feelings and wishes hidden even from ourselves. If someone tries to invade this area of privacy, we become anxious and build our defenses higher. Or if we open ourselves out of coercion, we then build up resentments against the intruder. Often our prayers are shallow because we cannot permit even God to enter the area of ourselves which we wish to conceal.

With this deep sense of privacy, we live in a community of persons. Our very personhood depends on our relationships with others. There is no way we can fulfill our destiny as persons by isolated self-manipulation, even though we would like to do so. Our destiny is to become part of others and permit others to become part of us. This is community, Christian community, to which the alternative is emotional and spiritual impoverishment. As persons, then, we have a deep need for privacy, for exercising the prerogative of individuality to set its own boundaries. But we also live in a community of persons.

For growth, health, and fulfillment the dimension of privacy needs to function in the direction of openness to ourselves, to others, and to God. Openness is the opposite of defensiveness, and is grounded in trust. Trust, according to Erikson, is learned in infancy, in the first stage of growth. It is only through openness that we can take in, assimilate, utilize, or discard what others have to give to us. To become a person is to live in tension between the need for privacy and the need to be open, a tension which is continually being overcome by trust. The growing person learns to test the power of reality to inflict emotional injury, to take certain risks of being hurt, to stake out less and less of himself as private, and to develop increasing openness and transparency before others. An effective pastor, through the quality of his relationships, enables others to lower their defenses and become increasingly open. This may be a problem for the pastor, since his privacy is constantly being intruded upon, and he may respond negatively to others for this reason. Also, openness may be pushed to a pathological degree through the compulsion to exhibit our emotional and spiritual anatomy as a means of manipulating others.

The kind of love manifest in Christ was a self-giving love, not a demanding, manipulative, possessive, or controlling love. This is the kind of love which makes it possible for others to be open to us, that is, as open as the specific forces of their being permit them to be at any given moment. Not all persons could open themselves to Christ, and some will not be able to open themselves to any pastor, nor permit us to be open to them. But the meaning of Christian love is that a relationship is offered which accepts the other as a person. One thing such acceptance means that his privacy is respected. Acceptance on such terms helps to make it possible for him to respond with some degree of openness. Until he himself is ready, we cannot advance further without doing harm. At such times we need to learn to relax and trust in the work of the Holy Spirit, for the Holy Spirit functions at the point where persons are struggling to overcome their privacy and accept fellowship in a community. "Behold, I stand at the door and knock. If any man open the door I will come in and sup with him and he with me." This deep insight expresses respect for the privacy of the person, but it also emphasizes his need for fellowship, and it indicates that fellowship is available. The pastor mediates the redemptive love of God in a measure when he respects the privacy of a person while at the same time he offers something of himself in an understanding, accepting relationship. Only genuine openness on the part of the pastor will allay anxieties in others and enable them to become open to him.

Another dimension in which persons experience themselves is uniqueness. By uniqueness we do not mean a sense of superiority or grandiosity. Neither do we mean the kind of fantasy which some persons have of themselves—the man who prayed and thanked God that he was not like other men (Luke 18:9-14). These are pathological expressions.

Our uniqueness means that we are called to become ourselves before God, that we have the gift of life with all of its possibilities from God and the responsibility of developing this potential. Psychologists speak of individuation, which involves the achievement of uniqueness. Christian theology speaks about man's being created in the image of God, and the Gospels about investing and multiplying one's talents. However we describe it, each person has a uniqueness that he is called upon to fulfill.

But we have this uniqueness along with much in common with other persons. In many ways we are very much alike. We live in a culture which pressures us into conformity, which in turn leads us to deny our individuality. Because of our common characteristics there can be a science and a theology of man. But our uniqueness cannot be formulated or generalized. It is not to be found in any book. It is to be found only in a living experience in which our relationship with ourselves, with others, and with God constantly calls us to change and growth. And this involves at times considerable renunciation and pain.

The need for becoming oneself, for fulfilling our uniqueness in some degree, is recognized by many today. It is stressed by Carl Rogers[5] in his book *On Becoming a Person*. It is also emphasized by existentialists like Rollo May[6] and, in terms of the concept of self-actualization, it is central in the formulations of Maslow.[7] But fulfilling one's uniqueness, or finding self-actualization, is not something to be achieved in isolation, but only in relationship with others. We become ourselves only in and through others and they become themselves only in and through us. The mother finds a part of her uniqueness through her child, and the child through the mother. This is emphasized by Paul Tillich[8] when he speaks of becoming oneself both as an individual and as a member of the group. Individuality and community are the two poles of self-realization, and these are always in dynamic tension. Psychoanalysis is an elaborate system for interpreting the intricacies of this process. In Christian theology the individual is seen in relation to the fellowship of the Church, the Christian community, and the Kingdom of God. The Christian faith, with its emphasis on the relationships of individuals before God, is equipped to recognize and foster uniqueness.

The redemptive, self-giving love which is in Christ respects the need for every man to become himself, that is, to develop his uniqueness, or to fulfill his potential. Redemptive love does not pressure persons into conformity of action or belief. It recognizes that we do not have the answers for the questions and problems of others; we may, however, have the power to relate to others in a way which helps them to find their own answers, to find the truth which is themselves before God. This is living truth, a truth manifested in relationships. This is life in the Spirit, not in the law. Amid all of the pressures of conformity in our culture, the Christian pastor should offer a relationship which opens the possibility for persons to become themselves before God. It is tragic when a church and its pastors so reinforce the static expectancies of our culture, that a young person, struggling with the problem of becoming himself can say, "All of my life I have had to be what others—my parents, teachers, pastor, and others—said I should be, so that now I do not know who I am or who I want to be. I only know I do not want to be what others tell me I should be." Christian experience calls men, not to conformity to this world, but to a kind of transformation that comes from the constant renewing of the mind and spirit in growing commitment to the Spirit of God. Again, only the pastor who is genuinely advancing toward becoming his real self before others and before God will be able to communicate to others, particularly to children and youth, the strength which will enable them to become themselves before God. Such a pastor will also arouse considerable hostility in those who are rigidly anxious and who alleviate their anxiety by conforming. But as he learns to deal with hostility in love and understanding, he will become part of the redemptive process in some of these persons also.

A third dimension of persons is awareness. Awareness involves a sensitivity to our own inner world and to the external world, including other persons. Through awareness we bring into consciousness the meaning of our relationships and experiences; we know them in a direct, living sense, and hence we are able to cope with negative meaning and to enhance positive meaning. Awareness is a direct knowledge of the living truth at work within us, as distinguished from knowledge about ourselves. Awareness involves insight, and insight is grounded in strength and trust. It is through awareness that a person fulfills his capacity for self-acceptance, self-understanding, and self-transcendence.

Awareness is developed very gradually from birth. At some time during the first year of life the infant becomes aware of others as distinct from himself. Mothers see the first signs of such awareness. Awareness of the self, of others, and of the meaning of experiences in relation to others is stimulated by satisfaction of needs at the hands of others, and also by frustration, conflict, and suffering. Such negative experiences may bring so much pain that the child turns away in denial and fantasy. The growing self is crippled to the extent that this happens. But awareness is an essential aspect of the self, and the self grows in part through becoming aware. The pastor constantly meets persons who are struggling to become aware of themselves, their motivations, the meaning of their relationships, and especially the meaning of their suffering, but who also find strong tendencies in themselves to avoid awareness.

A person, then, does not have to become aware. Freud shocked the world when he introduced his concept of repression. What is repression? It is a re-action of the self in which memories, feelings, and meanings are blotted out of consciousness; it is a blocking of the process of awareness. Awareness admits the raw material of life into consciousness, while repression pushes it back. Repression operates when the self is too weak to deal with issues or when aspects of experience are too painful. But memories, feelings, and meanings of which we are unconscious may seriously influence our existence. Indeed, this is part of the meaning of neurotic illness—the reactions of persons are being determined by memories and feelings of which he is not aware and hence does not understand and cannot control. Neurotic symptoms are expressions of repressed, unconscious material that has gained control in some disguised, symbolic form. Thus awareness is necessary to the control and direction of ourselves as persons. It also plays a significant part in our religious experience. Before we pray to be forgiven for our sins, for example, we should pray for strength to become aware of what our real sins are. We cannot confess what we are not aware of!

The depth of awareness of our relationships and their meaning forms the basis of our responses. For awareness, or insight, is our response; it is the way in which we take in meaning, assimilate it, and act upon it. This is at least part of what Tillich[9] seems to mean when he talks about taking anxiety into oneself. The obstacle to taking anxiety into the self is the pain involved. But the self gains in strength as it is able to become aware of its negative feelings and deal constructively with them. This means courageously facing the threatening forces within one's being and within one's relationships with others.

The psychologist is likely to speak of perception rather than of awareness. The difference is that perception is an operational psychological concept, while awareness is in the experience of a person. The problem of perception and its relation to personality factors is receiving much attention today. To what extent do personality factors such as feeling or desire color our preception of our inner and our external worlds? Distortions of perception are especially likely to occur where strong feeling such as fear, hate, or love is involved. The problem of preception is important to communication since it focuses attention on the way in which communication is received, and on why communications are often misunderstood. Perception is another way of formulating the problem of awareness.

From the experimental and clinical study of perception comes some confirmation of ideas held by several representatives of the dynamic point of view. Witkin[10] and his associates, in *Personality through Perception*, report the results of some experimental research in perception. They define the function of perception as that of separating an item from its field or context. Individual differences in the ability to separate an item from its context are related to the aggressive or passive character of the personality structure. Individuals who are dependent in their interpersonal relations are "field dependent" in their perceptual functioning, while those who are more aggressive and independent perceive objects more independently of the field. The authors describe these persons as follows:

Field-dependent persons tend to be characterized by passivity in dealing with the environment; by unfamiliarity with and fear of their own impulses, together with poor control over them; by lack of self-esteem; and by the possession of a relatively primitive, undifferentiated body image. Independent or analytically perceptual performers, in contrast, tend to be characterized by activity and independence in relation to the environment; by closer communication with, and better control of, their own impulses; and by relatively high self-esteem and more differentiated mature, body image.

These findings tend to confirm the general thesis that personality functions as a whole, and that the patterns of response which operate on one level tend to operate on all levels. A man's perception of objects and his perception of persons and values do not follow essentially different patterns. Perception and response are governed by the same needs, defenses, and self-image. Indeed, perception is part of the response, since it is the individual's own creation of his world, partly in terms of his own needs. There is a sense in which we create our world after our own image, a replica of our own unconscious. Or in other words, our perceived world becomes a smybol through which our own unconscious meanings, values, and prejudices, anxieties, guilts, and confusions, find expression.

The pastor will deal with many persons who are searching for awareness of meaning in their lives. Some will be very dependent and want quick and easy answers, and the pastor will be tempted to give such answers. But he will soon find that such answers are of little avail, for while they may be understood and accepted intellectually, they are powerless to penetrate to the deeper levels of being. Other persons will be in conflict, they will both want and not want to achieve insight. They will want it in so far as they want relief from their suffering, but they will not want it in so far as it involves their facing their suffering and coming to some kind of terms with it. Particularly difficult for them will be the kind of insight that reveals their attitudes toward themselves and others which they feel the need to justify or defend. Only through patience and understanding will the pastor be able to help such people, since they will perceive him also in terms of their own needs and patterns. It is for this reason that at times a long, self-giving relationship is necessary in order to help a person correct his own misperceptions of the pastor, or of others, from within. One of the goals of psychotherapy is the increase of awareness.

The problem of perception or awareness has real importance for the communication of the Gospel. Involved in such communication is not only the awareness of the pastor, how he perceives himself and the Gospel and those to whom he speaks, but also the factors which control the awareness of his hearers. Often the message proclaimed verbally is received and perceived by the hearers in a quite different manner than was intended. We hear and see what we are emotionally ready to hear and see.

Jesus faced and struggled with the problem of the level of awareness, and of handicaps to clear perception in those with whom he dealt. He sought to help men to gain insight into their

attitudes toward themselves, toward others, and toward God; but
he found it very difficult. When he spoke in parables his disciples
asked him for an explanation of the meaning, a common defense
against insight. He spoke of their having their hearts hardened;
that is, they could not be aware of what they were feeling nor of
the factors controlling their preceptions. Seeing, they did not see;
and hearing, they did not hear; nor did they understand. It is
only through seeing, hearing, and understanding on the deeper
levels of our being that we are healed.

Certainly one of the goals of pastoral care is to help persons
gain a deeper awareness of themselves and of their relationship
to others and to God, both actual and potential. This involves
insight into their inner conflicts, and how they tend to use others
in a manipulative, controlling manner. It also involves an awareness of the dimension of sin and its problems—not in the abstract, but in its concrete manifestation in their experience. But
it would need to go beyond this, and help persons to awareness of
the meaning of salvation in terms of love toward God and man.
In accomplishing this, the depth of awareness or insight of the
pastor will be a determining factor; his own lack of insight will
get in his way. But when he becomes concerned with what he is
communicating through his relationships, and measures his words
in this light, he will begin to help persons find strength. A Christian church ought to be a place where persons are expanding
their awareness of meaning, not a place where repression is encouraged. It is through awareness that the Holy Spirit functions
to lead men into truth.

A fourth dimension of persons which is significant for pastoral
care is autonomy.

By autonomy we do not mean "absolute" freedom. As we study
human life we cannot help but become aware of the numerous
levels of the determinants—biological, psychological, social,
philosophical—which to a measure control our behavior either in
a positive or a negative fashion.[11] But even from the biological
sciences comes evidence that a living organism possesses spontaneity, that is, the ability to control its responses from within
itself to act on its environment as well as to react to its environment.

Interpreters of human behavior from an existential[12] point of

view understand the potential for autonomy as an inherent element in man's existence. Psychotherapeutic psychology seems to
be very deterministic in its formulations, but it assumes sufficient
autonomy on the part of the patient to permit him the decision
to move into therapy, and to make certain necessary decisions
about himself along the way. Christian theology[13] has held to a
large element of freedom, but it has not been blind to deterministic elements in man.

The tendency to put antonomy and determinism in opposi-
tion, where accepting one concept means rejecting the other, is
mistaken. Personal existence is lived in a tension between these
opposites. Perhaps it would be more accurate to say that a man is
determined by many inner and external forces, but that he also
has the potential for autonomy. Paul (Gal. 6:7) insisted on freedom in Christ, but it was he who wrote, "Whatever a man sows,
that he will also reap." Here he is speaking deterministically.
Today we could reinterpret that sentence and add, whatever is
sown in a child, that will he reap in later life. The potential for
autonomy is developed through experience, and many children
are denied the kind of human relationships which make this
possible. They become adults with the inability to act autono-
mously, or at least with a low degree of functioning autonomy.
To the extent that a person has failed to develop autonomy or
has lost it, he is sick. The pastor needs to sense the limits of a
person's ability to exercise his autonomy, and not expect of him,
at a given moment, a level of autonomous behavior of which he
is not capable. It is also the function of the Christian faith to
help persons expand the functioning limits of their autonomy.

Since autonomy is a function of the human ego, the next question is that of the nature of the ego, considered both psychologically and theologically.

Theologically it is often assumed that the ego, or self, is bad.
This is often interpreted to be the meaning of Jesus' statements
about self-denial (Matt. 16:25). In these intrepretations the self
is often considered as evil, a thing to be denied. Such interpretations fail to make a very necessary distinction, probably because
they grow out of a basic antagonism toward pleasurable impulses
in man. These objections are really aimed at an aspect of persons
which is expressed in Freud's term "narcissism," which means an

infantile feeling of self-love, worth, and power, and the need to organize the entire universe around oneself. Freud pointed out that the process of growth consists in part in giving up a large measure of narcissism and learning to relate to objects, particularly to other persons, in terms of themselves. In this sense certain infantile aspects of the self do need to be denied or renounced, in order that a person may grow to more mature levels. The potential for this growth is inherent in the real ego or self, but requires certain qualities of human relationship for fulfillment. To help persons understand the necessity for giving up immature satisfactions for the sake of more mature experiences is sound. Or to help them see that commitment to Christ involves denying or modifying those aspects of the self which are in conflict with the spirit of Christ is also sound. But to preach that they must deny the real self and become "selfless" is to teach persons that they must be less than human—puppets either on the strings of their own unconscious impulses or of some environmental power.

But the real issue between Christian theological and modern psychological concepts of the ego or self is on a different point. For Christian theology[15] holds to a nonempirical self, a self transcendent to experience while partaking in experience, a given out of which growth occurs.

On the other hand, psychological theories[16] of the self have been empirical, their content depending on specific points of view. In Freud's thought, for example, the ego becomes differentiated as the infant finds himself in conflict between his impulses and external reality, and the function of the ego is to test reality and to discover some kind of solution of the conflict. In the infant the ego is considered very weak, and its growth depends upon wholesome relationships and the resolution of conflict. With the development of the superego, the ego faces the new task of reconciling impulses and wishes with demands and prohibitions. Here is some of the origin of intrapsychic conflict; the other part beign the possibility of conflict between elements of the ego itself.

There would seem to be no question as to the empirical nature of ego development. This means that the way in which a person functions in perceiving inner or external reality, his ability to test this reality and to relate to it in terms of its demands and also his own needs, his ability to project solutions of his conflict in his imagination, his ability to make decisions and carry them out in action—these and other such capacities are the product of learning. Indeed, Sullivan[17] would define the self in terms of "security operations"; that is, the self develops out of the need for the person to master anxiety.

It should be noted here that the experience of conflict and evil is central in both the Christian and the Freudian account of the self. The Biblical account of creation in Genesis sees man's awareness emerging out of conflict between aspects within himself (Adam debated whether or not he should eat the apple) and between himself and his Creator. The empirical point of view disregards ultimate relationships but understands the ego to emerge through conflict with other persons, beginning with the mother, and it sees the conflicts here in terms both of those which are inevitable because of the human situation and of those produced because of immaturities within the mother. In other words, on either level the problem of the ego is the problem of relationships, both what it receives and how it responds, and how it deals with conflict. The ego is the totality of those processes which seek to synthesize inner needs and conflicts with outer demands, frustrations, and value. The self is the ego subjectively experienced.

But there is a growing tendency today in psychological circles to consider a nonempirical aspect of the self. Karen Horney[18] describes "the real self as that central inner force, common to all human beings yet unique in each, which is the deep source of growth."

Several psychoanalysts, of which Heinz Hartmann[19] is a leader, have expanded Freud's theory of the ego to make room for a "conflict-free" aspect of the ego which functions according to its own spontaneous nature. In other words, here is a concept of ego functions which exist prior to conflict and are not dependent upon conflict for their functioning.

Hartmann begins with a period prior to the experience of conflict, when the ego and the id are still undifferentiated. The ego thus partakes of the hereditary factors which are recognized as the root of instinctive drives. Hartmann believes that the ego and its functions (perception, motility, memory, thinking) are grounded on laws of maturation which are part of their nature and not derived from the instincts. While relationships and conflicts with the external world are seen to play a large part in the actual growth of the ego, yet there is still a "conflict-free" portion which functions according to its own laws. These "autonomous factors" are termed "primary ego autonomy." But the ego may find itself in conflict, and to resolve the conflict may utilize the defense mechanism of reaction formation, for example, and adopt the attitude of altruism to cover up deep feelings of resentment. Later, the conflict may be resolved, but the attitude of altruism remains. This Hartman calls "secondary autonomy," and he considers it a highly important process in the development of the stability of personality. The same "secondary autonomy" may occur in relation to other defense mechanisms. Or the opposite may occur, and the ego may hold onto destructive behavior after the original conflict which produced the behavior has been resolved. The problem here is that of the reversibility and irreversibility of structure. It is important to note that Hartmann considers the synthetic or integrating function of the ego to belong to that area which is governed by primary autonomy.

Autonomy of the ego is not to be confused with conscious self-direction or rational choice, although these may be involved. On the other hand, much that passes for rational decision may be really pseudo-autonomy. For example, an individual acting under a strong compulsion may insist that he is acting out of autonomy. Autonomous integrating functions operate on a level deeper than rational processes, and the person is conscious, not that he is integrating himself, but that integration is taking place within him. He experiences this as something being done to him rather than as something he is doing. And yet he also recognizes this change as something which is the result of processes within himself, and which for him is a valid and authentic experience. He does not see it as due to outside control, just as he does not see it as the result of a conscious decision.

In such experiences the person may be aware of a new mastery of his impulses, or perhaps of a modification of some overscrupulous part of his conscience. A kind of impulsive behavior, for example, which has been a problem no longer occurs. Or he may be aware of a new strength and a fresh approach to a reality problem; a new way of relating, for example, to authority figures which had previously given him problems. This new strength and its resulting change of behavior is experienced not as the result of his own conscious effort but as being received. There is also a new sense of responsibility, meaning the ability to respond in depth in a constructive rather than in a destructive manner in personal relationships.

The relation of these interpretations to certain of those in Christian experience should not be missed. For there is much in Christian literature, and in the writings of the mystics,[20] which sounds strangely like the experience of ego autonomy, even though it is expressed in other terms. The Christian understanding has been that any changes taking place within a person are not the result of his conscious will (no man can save himself), but rather the result of God working within him. Sometimes these changes are attributed to the work of the Holy Spirit, or God in us. Yet the testimony has been that a man is most free or autonomous when he is most obedient to God. Only in a legalistic, compulsive type of religion is God understood as a being who reduces man's freedom.

Genuine love toward God and toward self and others, when it is experienced, releases autonomous powers within the individual, and a new sense of strength and changed relationships are the result.

The communication of the Gospel, or pastoral care, always needs to be given within the context of the autonomy of both the communicator and the recipient. The level of freedom or autonomy possessed by a pastor will guide the amount of autonomy he will be able to allow others. The pastor who is compulsively determined in his attitudes and relationships will seek to bring others under his authority. The meaning of love, as we reveal it in our relationships, will be in part expressed in the quality of autonomy we are able to grant to others. The pastor may find himself in real conflict between authoritative and autonomous principles.

On the other hand, the pastor will deal with persons who are not, at a given moment, inwardly free to accept the love of God, or any relationship which involves autonomy. They will understand God in authoritative, demanding terms, and will need a relationship on the human level to make the possibility of autonomous experience real to them. In their inability to be autonomous they will find themselves unable to make a fully Christian decision. Christian decisions which are made through pressures from others represent a pseudo autonomy and will lead to a neurotic condition if adhered to.

Part of the meaning of the grace of God is that men have the freedom to accept or reject what is given. Grace is never forced. For grace, which is God's free gift to men, given out of God's abundance and man's need, respects man as an autonomous person. Too many persons in our churches have made their decisions about the Christian faith out of fear or guilt and have not experienced a positive motivation in their religious life. Pastoral care is genuinely effective when it permits a person to come to himself and to make the decision which concerns his eternal destiny from within himself.

The pastor is called upon to minister to persons caught in a culture that has developed strong pressures toward conformity, and at times to minister to persons caught in various forms of rebellion. Sometimes the Church itself is organized to enforce conformity; it has the powerful sanctions of guilt and punishment, and sometimes promises of salvation in return for conformity. Sometimes the Church is expected to reinforce patterns of conformity set by groups in the larger culture.

The pastor may see himself as an official enforcer of conformity and defender of fixed standards, "the conscience of the community." Or he may feel the pressures of his congregation, or of his denominational body, or of his local community forcing him into conformity. One of the strong professional hazards of young clergymen today is the temptation to deny their individuality by conforming to standards set by powerful groups. To the extent that the pastor becomes a victim of this pressure—and most of us do at some point—he becomes powerless to help others caught in the same web. While rebellion may save him from the evils of conformity, it has its own dangers and inadequacies. The Christian faith calls for the development of human potential in positive ways, through love and service and sacrifice and courage. Only as the pastor has found this path can he lead others over it.

And he needs to see his task here on both the individual and the group level. In a unique way the pastor stands between the individual and his culture and is called upon to mediate health and wholeness to each.

The Christian understanding of the meaning of grace takes us into the very heart of human nature. For part of the idea of grace involves the close dependence of man on his Creator for life and sustenance, and on his Redeemer for an understanding and experience of the kind of relationships which brings fulfillment of himself as a creature. When man forgets he is a creature, dependent on the grace of God, he forges for himself an identity in which he seeks to become God. But on the other hand, when man experiences the meaning of dependence on God as a person and not as a thing, and understands that part of the gift of grace is the gift of autonomy or freedom, and that accepting the grace of God means fulfilling one's autonomy, then the idea of dependence on God takes on a creative meaning. It is not dependence as usually practiced in human relationships, where the dependent individual neurotically surrenders his autonomy. It is a relationship in which one recognizes God as the source of his being and all that fulfills that being, including the power of decision. The doctrine of grace thus symbolizes the tremendous dependence of man on God, and in the light of man's autonomy it also symbolizes the interdependence of persons, rather than dependence on others. Experiences akin to grace may occur on the human level when we receive from others love that may be accepted without surrendering autonomy. But there is always the ambiguous element in human relations which is not present in the grace of God.

We have been speaking of a situation which is paradoxical. When a person experiences autonomy in depth, it is as though what is happening to him is a gift rather than the result of his own effort. Yet this is experienced as autonomy, or freedom. It is this experience which D. M. Baillie[21] calls the "paradox of grace."

Baillie points out that whenever through faith we understand God as the ultimate source of anything in our experience, "He comes in, as it were, on the vertical line from the eternal world to touch the horizontal line on which we inevitably have another explanation in empirical terms."[22] The Incarnation is the central paradox, he holds, since in it we see the life of God Himself, but also a completely human life. Baillie's statement of the paradoxical nature of the Christian faith is important for our interpretation of pastoral care, since we are saying that it is the task of the pastor to communicate the Gospel to persons at the point of both their ultimate and proximate needs. If the Christian faith has any meaning, it must be found in relation to the needs of personal existence. Any attempt to understand the relation between the Christian faith and modern psychotherapy must take this paradoxical situation into account; and it must recognize that beyond all formulations there is a mystery in faith which is beyond knowledge and which therefore resists all attempts at formulation.

Of the paradox of grace, Baillie writes, "Its essence lies in the conviction which a Christian man possesses, that every good thing in him, every good thing he does, is somehow not wrought by himself but by God. This is a highly paradoxical conviction, for in ascribing all to God it does not abrogate human personality nor disclaim personal responsibility. Never is human action more truly and fully personal, never does the agent feel more perfectly free, than in those moments of which he can say as a Christian that whatever good was in them was not his but God's."[23] Paul's statement is taken as a classical expression of this paradox: "By the grace of God I am what I am, and his grace toward me was not in vain. On the contrary, I worked harder than any of them, though it was not I, but the grace of God which is with me" (I Cor. 15:10).

The paradox of grace is an expression of the faith of the Christian that the good which he achieves is somehow not through his own efforts, but through a creative energy or power which was given to him. The Christian feels himself free and responsible, and accepts failure as his own doing, but he sees whatever good he accomplishes as the working of God's power within him. Furthermore, he is not anxious at the demands of God, for he understands that God asks nothing that He does not also give the grace to fulfill.

The experience in which the paradox of grace becomes real cannot be produced in us by verbal descriptions of it. It is experienced in an I-Thou relationship with God in which a person responds to God's self-giving love in wonder and gratitude, and is able to accept himself in the light of God's acceptance of him. This does not mean that he becomes a perfect person, but living under the experience of grace should enable him to face, accept, and deal realistically with weaknesses. Grace never excuses us from responsibility; indeed, it placed responsibility on us. Nor should we use our freedom to perpetuate destructive trends. Grace may bring to our awareness certain problems which we can work out only with the help of others, but this help will be accepted also as an expression of the grace of God. Thus it is not a weakness for a Christian to seek psychological or pastoral help. And the pastor who would give this help must be able to communicate grace and at the same time know how to deal with the empirical aspects of experience.

Earlier we indicated some possible objections to our interpretation of the work of the pastor as mediating the grace of God. One objection is that this concept is presumptuous; no human being can mediate God's grace. Behind this objection there is the tendency to discount or degrade the meaning of human relationships. This tendency can be very real and highly important to some persons because of harmful experiences with others who professed to love them. But the mediation of the grace of God does not require perfection in the pastor. Furthermore, it can never be done except from within the paradox of grace: I, yet not I, but the grace of God. As soon as we see ourselves as mediating God's love under our own power, we fail in communication. When we see that which we are able to be in relation to another as genuinely ourselves, yet not of ourselves, then some measure of the ultimate meaning of persons will be communicated with the immediate meaning.

Today there is emphasis on the "role of the minister," and some studies have indicated considerable confusion as to what the role of the minister really is. But there is a much deeper problem, and that is the profound fear in many ministers of the kind of spontaneous relationships with persons in which needs are felt and responses must be given. Because of this fear, ministers are inclined to "define their role" in the hope that clear definition will give a basis for action without the necessity of exposing themselves. But role-playing of this kind does not lead to genuine communication of the Gospel. In its exaggerated forms such role-playing becomes playing God. The emptiness and futility of this is apparent. When the pastor forgets his "role" and learns to give himself—however little he has—genuinely, honestly, and spontaneously, as God gave himself in Christ, then the Gospel will become a living issue to his people. Fear of honest spontaneity in human relationships is basically fear of the Holy Spirit and of its power in human life. It is the letter, the role, that kills; but the Spirit gives life.

We began this chapter with the questions, What is man? and Who is a person? The secret of communicating the Gospel to persons at the point of their need is to meet them as persons in a relationship in which the paradoxical conditions of grace and personal responsibility find expression. We have not exhausted the dimensions of personal existence, but we have spoken of privacy, uniqueness, awareness, and autonomy as important in the process of being and becoming. The Gospel must be communicated within these dimensions. This challenges the pastor to learn the meaning of these dimensions in his own experience as a person. He will then have a basis for knowing what they mean to others.

What is man? We go to psychology and to Christian theology for answers to this question. Who is a person? Here we can not depend on generalizations; we must go to the person himself, in an understanding, mutually revealing relationship. A person is the only creature who is aware that he lives in two worlds at the same time—the empirical and the ultimate. This dual orientation characterizes the unique potential of a person. It is not enough to communicate verbally the Christian answers to the questions arising in such an existence. The person must be met as a person, a Who, whether individually or in a group, and in the kind of relationship which mediates something of the nature and meaning of God to his empirical condition, whatever that happens to be. This is the meaning of pastoral care, the act of caring for persons in the spirit of Christ.

※ 4 ※
Further Considerations

THE concept of pastoral care as developed by Eduard Thurneysen in *A Theology of Pastoral Care* is in direct contrast to the one we are developing. To Thurneysen, pastoral care means conversation. Its content is the same as the content of preaching, "a specific communication to the individual of the message proclaimed in general (i.e., to all) in the sermon to the congregation."[1] It is based on preaching, and leads back to it. It is the communication of the "Word of God," a concept which appears constantly, and often with a vagueness of meaning, in Thurneysen's book. Essentially it seems to mean the content of his particular theology, for it soon becomes evident that the pastoral care of Roman Catholicism and of Pietism is totally unacceptable because it is grounded in different theologies. Pastoral counseling is "listening to the Word of God and responding to the Word of God."[2] Psychology is important for listening to a person, but immediately the pastor must challenge human meaning by questions directed from the Word of God. Listening is not for the sake of understanding the person but rather for the sake of gaining a vantage point from which to make a theological critique. This is described as the "breach" in the pastoral conversation—the analysis of human meaning in the light of the Word of God, that is, according to the theological beliefs of the pastor.

Thurneysen has trouble with the human side of pastoral care. He agrees that man must accept and respond to the Gospel, yet under the transcendent sovereignty of God man can do nothing for himself. The pastor cannot speak the Word through his own efforts or thought: "he does not speak out of his own depths, but he speaks with all the power given him by that alien Word now conferred upon him; he speaks the Word of God."[3]

The pastoral relationship is not an important consideration for Thurneysen. Pastoral conversation is the central element in his approach. The relationship is left largely to implication. The pastor is interested, sympathetic, and concerned for the person. He sees himself as standing under the same judgment as the person, an idea which is shared by other points of view. However, the relationship is an adjunct of the pastoral conversation rather than, as we are interpreting it, the basis for the conversation.

Not until the final chapter does Thurneysen discuss the relationship as such. This relationship becomes one of mutual trust through the word of forgiveness under which both pastor and person stand in relation to God. The great danger, he holds, is that of mutual dependence. Pastoral care must avoid any human dependence since this may stand in the way of the one valid dependence, dependence on God. Here Thurneysen identifies dependence with transference in the psychological sense. He admits that such dependences may be unavoidable, and indicates that when they occur they must be recognized and dissolved. But he does not indicate how they are to be used for the benefit of the person. He makes no distinction between real and neurotic dependence, and nowhere in his discussion does he mention autonomy. He seeks to bind the person to God rather than to aid him in outgrowing neurotic dependence and becoming autonomous. There is little room for human autonomy in his theological position.

There is no question but that the point of emphasis in Thurneysen's formulations is on the spoken word of the pastor, not on the person to whom he is speaking. The person is very secondary in importance; he is manipulated, theologically indoctrinated, and made dependent on the authority of the pastor. There is a kind of theological overintellectualization here which makes deep insight unnecessary. And one cannot escape the feeling that there is great dependence on the magic of words. Listening takes place in the light of the pastor's theology, not in terms of the meaning of existence to the person who is speaking. The stress of pastoral care is on guilt and forgiveness. We would accept this as very important, but not as the whole concern of the Gospel with the needs of persons.

Thurneysen's interpretation of pastoral care is the logical outgrowth of his theological position. A rigid emphasis on the transcendent sovereignty of God and the nothingness of man, on the alien nature of God in his relation to man, and on the power of verbal symbols seems to characterize his position. Such a position, if one can subscribe to it, does remove certain anxieties about the human situation and lift the despair created by fully accepted human responsibility. It also reduces a man to a puppet in the hands of the pastor and thus destroys his autonomy. An individual is placed in the terrible position of rejecting God if he rejects the words of the pastor. But he is also given reassurance that acceptance of verbal formulations will guarantee him eternal salvation.

Pastoral care, as we are developing it here, involves conversation, but more than conversation. Conversation, or dialogue,[4] is grounded in a relationship that makes such communication possible. In many pastoral conversations there is no real communication, or the communication may be negative. Communication in depth takes place when one enters into the experience of another person in terms of its meaning to him, and within this relationship, says what is helpful or remains silent as the situation requires. Furthermore, it is not some kind of an "alien Word" which persons need for growth or redemption. It is the sense of the presence of a God who in Christ has involved himself in the joys, the struggles, the suffering, and the destiny of human beings by becoming incarnate and fully participating in human existence. While the pastor's faith must be strong and redemptive, his theological formulations must be subject to examination in the light of what he learns from human experience, or else they are likely to be used in an unhealthy manner.

In the field of psychotherapy we can observe an intellectual approach very similar to that of Thurneysen, although different in content. Some psychotherapists, representing different schools, place great emphasis on the intellectual interpretation of a client's experiences in psychological terms. These therapists will place little emphasis on the feeling and meaning aspects of a patient's experience. The result is that the patient is likely to emerge from such therapy with a full indoctrination, fully committed to certain verbal formulations, but with his problems still unresolved. Such patients can discuss human conflicts and problems, but they are very poor in their relationships with others. Fortunately, this seems to be true of a decreasing number of therapists. Our point here is that it makes little difference whether the content be psychological or theological, the result is very similar. The individual finds his security in a system of verbal formulations rather than in a growing ability to enter into human relationships through trust and love. He learns to live on the theories of others rather than on his own insights and understanding.

According to Henry J. Cadbury, the method of Jesus was quite the opposite. He says, "The kind of knowledge Jesus looked for was not so much imparted information as insight achieved. There is in fact reason to suppose that he did not refer so often to what his followers were to be told as to what they were to recognize and to discover. . . . Jesus' complaint is that men do not recognize the implications of their attitudes. But this is something you cannot simply tell them. It requires understanding, perception or insight."[5] And we might add that such insight is fostered through a relationship of deep trust and acceptance.

Pastoral conversation, grounded in a relationship of acceptance and understanding in which the pastor becomes involved in the feelings and meanings of others, is aimed at enabling others to experience insight and understanding from within themselves. They learn to understand their actual relationship with themselves, with others, and with God, to discover the results of these relationships in terms of themselves and others, to find the questions raised by their situation and experience, and to discover for themselves their own answers in the light of the Gospel. The real pastor does not have preconceived questions or answers. It is the experience of reality rather than acceptance of verbal formulations in which he is interested since such reality is the source of growth and fulfillment.

This seems to limit the formal use of theological concepts in pastoral care. Indeed, this is sometimes the case, depending upon the function that the pastor is performing at the moment. Preaching and teaching are impossible without the use of theological concepts; in some other forms of pastoral care these concepts need not play such a prominent part. Indeed, in some instances the pastor communicates only those concepts which would be healing or redemptive to the person immediately involved. But in all forms of pastoral care the concepts he offers will be empty and meaningless unless he is present with the person or group in the spirit of redemptive love.

This relationship of theology to pastoral care is recognized by the theologian, Carl Michalson. In his book, *Faith for Personal Crises,*[6] he says,

The theology which is being done in this volume is, I believe, what might be called a poimenical theology, a theology for the proper shepherding of sheep. (The Greek word, poimen, is the word for shepherd.) Restricting the scope of the treatment to the personal crises in the lives of the people, it is simply one branch of the care of souls. I have called that branch a theology for crucial situations. Unlike the traditional forms of theology, such as Biblical, historical and dogmatic theology, it does not need to say everything there is to say about the faith. It says only what is immediately pertinent to the situations at hand. It may even deliberately soft-pedal some elements in the total body of belief which might obstruct the healing process. It has the aim of relieving rather than intensifying the crisis. It will not deal in magnitudes of knowledge, for what is needed in a crucial situation is not true propositions but an understanding of one's life. Nor will it become authoritarian and directive, insisting on the truth of its claims. There is just no point to that. Under conditions of crisis the truth must validate itself, entering as a liberating perspective. There is only one test of truth within a crucial situation: Does it illuminate and heal? Even that test cannot be applied before the therapeutic process has set in.

Pastoral care should not be limited to events of crisis, but should see its tasks also in terms of the processes of growth, of being and becoming. However, we believe that the point made by Michalson is equally applicable to the broader concept, especially to certain expressions of it. Verbal formulations have their value, but they are powerless to create the experience to which they strive to give rational form. Such experiences are generated out of the potentialities of being when one person is associated with another in a relationship of self-giving love. When there is a trusting response to such love, a person is created or healed. The major difference between becoming ourselves through growth and becoming ourselves through healing in a moment of crisis is that in the first experience nothing has to be undone and redone. As pastors we should be as much concerned with this means of growth as with healing in crises.

The communication of the Gospel is therefore something more than the communication of verbal or logical concepts about the Gospel. The Gospel is concerned with man as *being*, as being before God, as being created and called into existence by God. The Gospel is concerned with the redemption of man through the restoration of the lost Image of God in which he was created. This redemption means calling man into his fulfillment, into his full measure of being. Such an experience reaches far deeper than the verbal and logical capacities of man. It reaches into those nonrational aspects of being out of which comes the power for being or the dread of being. It is on this level that man experiences himself as a person before God, or as a broken, guilt-laden, anxious individual seeking to escape from both himself and God. It is this level of being which responds in trust to grace and love, which experiences a sense of inner certainty, which senses meaning in personal relationships and responds accordingly. Ideas alone do not promote growth or healing on this level. Here ideas become real and elicit their appropriate responses only through the reality or relationships. John Calvin,[7] in spite of his emphasis on intellectual formulations, has written,

> For the Word of God is not received by faith if it floats on the surface of the brain; but when it has taken deep root in the heart, so as to become an impregnable fortress to sustain and repel temptation. But if it be that the right apprehension of the mind proceeds from the illumination of the Spirit, his energy is far more conspicuous in such confirmation of the heart . . . the furnishing of the heart with assurance being more difficult than the communication of knowledge to the understanding.

Genuine assurance arises from the nonrational, emotional depth of being and is authenticated by the spirit of trust and love. But there is a pseudo assurance prevalent which is a compulsive acceptance of verbal ideas without genuine inner authentication in being. Only in the quality of relationship that we have been describing can the creative and healing work of the Holy Spirit be manifest.

Pastoral Care and Pastoral Activities

Pastoral care, the communication of the Gospel to persons at their point of need primarily through relationships, should be distinguished from the activities through which it may be carried out. Preaching, religious education, church administration, calling, counseling, conducting worship, and other activities of the pastor are forms of pastoral care. But if these forms are engaged in by the pastor without a relationship of love and concern for persons, then they lead to ineffectiveness and disillusionment for both pastor and people. Actual harm may result when the pastor is too strongly motivated by negative feelings toward persons. Pastoral care, the participation of pastor and people in experiences through which the Gospel of redemption becomes real, must be genuinely motivated, or it is nothing. Furthermore, the work of the Holy Spirit through the pastor is not necessarily confined to the present forms. Perhaps in today's world we need some new forms through which redemptive participation can take place.

In recent years, at least one old form has been revived, that of hearing confessions, now referred to as pastoral counseling. The revival of this form has frightened many people for various reasons. Yet confession is inherent in the Gospel and in the Biblical witness, and there is profound need for it in human experience. It is a form of pastoral care that the Church must foster and develop far beyond its present scope, or we must surrender an essential ministry aimed at the deeper levels of human need to the so-called secular priests of healing. This will drive many who feel called to the ministry of healing out of the pastoral ministry, and lose others from the Church. The Church should rather develop the practice of pastoral counseling to the full, carefully delineating its values and limitations and the kind of training it requires. Pastoral counseling and professional psychotherapy should exist as two independent but co-operative professions, with deeper understanding developed between the representatives of both professions.

Pastoral counseling should not be identified with pastoral care, but this is one of the many forms of pastoral care. Counseling is a process by which a person communicates to the pastor on the level of deep personal feelings in order to work out or resolve a personal problem. When the need for conseling is at an end, the deeper aspects of the relationship of pastor and person are relinquished, since the pastor's responsibility is to help others resolve their dependence on him and become responsible toward God. Just what this means concretely depends on the needs of each person. All pastoral counseling ought to involve pastoral care, but not all pastoral care is carried on through counseling.

Pastoral care, as we are interpreting it, is more than a ministry to persons in crises. It is also a ministry to persons at the point of growth. This is in sharp contrast to previous concepts of pastoral care. Many human crises are unnecessary and could be prevented by proper care before the situation reaches critical dimensions; many could be forestalled by experiences which promote growth. On the other hand, not all human crises are preventable, since there are elements in the human situation which cannot be predicted or controlled. The deepest need of a human being is for relationships in which growth may take place. The kind of personal decision and commitment for which the Christian faith asks cannot be given unless a certain level of maturity has been reached. The experience of decision may be a crisis, and growth will be both a contributing factor to, and result of, its true resolution.

We have been describing pastoral care as a quality of relationship which should find expression in various pastoral activities. In considering pastoral activities more specifically, we shall be limited by the fact that elaboration of the point of view of this book on each of these activities would require a book in itself.

Preaching is a form of pastoral care; that is, it is a means through which the pastor attempts to speak to a congregation in terms of the meaning of the Gospel for human need. To say that preaching is proclamation is to state only half of the truth. The proclamation must be brought into dynamic relation to human need, or else we have only a dissertation on theology. As a dissertation it may be theologically acceptable, but also it may be completely meaningless to the congregation. Effective communication of the Gospel in preaching requires that the preacher speak out of a genuine experience of himself before God and before his fellow men, in which he has learned the meaning of self-giving love.

Preaching is indeed communication, and is always a two-way process. The preacher who speaks out of his theological knowledge alone will find himself engaging in a one-way declamation contest. His people cannot respond because they have not participated in theological study. But, the Gospel asks for much more than an intellectual response; it demands a response of faith which involves the whole man. If people are to respond, if there is to be conversation, their needs must be involved in the process of communication.

The Gospel is communicated in preaching only when the ideas and concepts of the sermon find a reality in the experience of both speaker and hearer. Thus the preacher may speak of the love of God while many in his congregation are thinking, "I can't believe that God really loves me. I wish I could believe this." These persons may feel this way because they did not know a genuine human love in childhood. For similar reasons some persons may accept the preacher's words superficially, but find no deep response to them. They may enjoy the sermon because it feeds their fantasy of being loved. Or the preacher may speak of trust, faith, forgiveness, or another theme, with the same result. Ideas and concepts are interpretations of the Gospel, and there is real communication only when the hearer and speaker experience the reality to which the ideas point.

Consider the preacher. He may speak of the love of God with anger in his voice, and if so, he communicates anger. He can speak of the forgiveness of God in a manner which leaves his congregation feeling more guilty, or reveals his own guilt. He may speak of faith and communicate his own anxiety. He may speak "with the tongues of men and of angels, but. . . ." It is rather amazing that through the centuries of preaching, much of it ineffective, preachers have been on the defensive rather than predisposed discover the roots of the problem. One form of defense has been the idealization of preaching through books and lectures. Another has been the kind of theological interpretation of preaching that places all the responsibility for effective communication on God or the Holy Spirit. While we would not minimize the Word of God or the work of the Holy Spirit, we are insisting that the quality of the relationship that the pastor creates with his people is one of the profound sources of effectiveness or ineffectiveness in preaching. The pastor's relationship blocks or provides a context for the work of the Spirit. Theological education needs to ponder the significance of this in terms of methodology in teaching young men to preach. We need to place less emphasis on courses dealing with the mechanics of preaching, and stress much more the approaches that will promote the growth of the preacher as a person.

Likewise, the Gospel may be embodied and portrayed in the institutional form which is the Church, but institutional forms are not the Gospel. The Church may be interpreted as the "Body of Christ" with so much attention given to the structural organization and program that the redemptive relationship is lost. The Gospel is a living reality which creates and sustains the institution, and which in turn may create and re-create persons through the medium of the institution. If the administrative functions of the Church are not used for their deeper pastoral purposes, they will be used for ends which are destructive of persons. The creative life of the minister himself is at stake in the same issue!

Again, the Gospel is much deeper than an abstract ethical ideal or the mores or cultural pattern of a particular community. Certainly, ethical ideals are involved in the life of any Christian, and many of the problems brought to the pastor will involve a conflict of ideals or a failure to meet ideals. However, the essence of the Gospel is not in an abstract description of human behavior, but lies in the deeper motivation from which the behavior springs. This is the meaning of Paul's insistence that love is the fulfillment of the law, and of the statement of Jesus that he came not to destroy the law but to fulfill it. A moral code never produced the fruits of the Spirit. It is possible unconsciously to commit spiritual suicide by doing the right acts for the wrong reasons. A mother may feed her infant in an attitude of genuine love, or she may do it in an attitude of pseudo love which covers up a deep rejection of the child. In each case the child will be fed, but the effect on the child will be the difference between healthy and neurotic growth. The preaching of ideals rather than the mediation of love may be an expression of our own unconscious guilt. Tragically, we have known this to be the case.

Again, the ritual and liturgy of worship are forms through which the relationship of the Gospel may be very effectively communicated in depth, or the attention of the priest and the worshipers may be kept on the surface. Ritual is composed of words, but also of acts through which the deep, inner meaning of the Gospel is portrayed. The task of the priest before the altar is to represent God to the people, and the people before God, and thus to act in the role of a mediator. The call "Lift up your hearts," used in so many services, may fall on ears deadened by external and internal pressures, so that no lifting up is possible. The result is emptiness and meaninglessness. Words and acts are present, but not the inner reality of the experience of worship. The deepest act of Christian worship occurs in the Holy Communion, where, through the concrete acts of eating and drinking, something of the Spirit of Christ and the meaning of his life may be taken into the worshiper. Such a service may be a profound ministry of pastoral care, but many persons will first need another form of pastoral care—that of confession or counseling—in order to work through the inner barriers to the kind of response that the Communion asks. Thus one form of pastoral care may be dependent on another and vice versa.

With some psychological and theological insight, the pastor may discover that overemphasis on form, be it rational, institutional, liturgical, or ethical, is in itself a kind of personality perversion and a kind of idolatry. Its aim is to protect the person from inner reality and truth which would provoke strong anxiety. As Jesus himself pointed out, and as confirmed in any textbook on abnormal psychology, form is very appealing as a substitute for inner reality. Religious forms may be used for concealment rather than for insight, especially when the content concerns the deeper, nonrational aspects of the person. The deepest communication of the Gospel is on the level of relationship which portrays and illuminates the Incarnation. Vital communication uses forms, but only for the purpose of mediating an inner spirit.

In Chapter I, I spoke of the disintegrating forces at work in the daily experience of the pastor. The integrating factor in the work of the pastor is not to be found in forms or activities as such, but in the reality of the Gospel which should be communicated to persons through those activities. Insofar as forms or activities serve other purposes—institutional, moralistic, or indoctrinational, for example—this deeper, integrating factor will not be present.

Having mentioned the Holy Communion, a word is in order in regard to the sacraments as the medium of communication of some aspect or quality of the grace of God. In addition to the theological understanding of the sacraments, the pastor must understand the psychological processes which condition or determine response of persons to them. He may observe situations of greatly overdetermined response which grow out of compulsive needs within a person or a group. An illustration of this is Luther's use of the confessional.[8] We have known Protestants to participate compulsively and ritualistically in the Holy Communion when they do not have the resource of the confessional. On the other hand, psychological factors may block a positive response to a sacrament, or create a strongly negative response. The pastor will learn about some of these factors if he makes this the subject of conversation when he calls on those parishioners who systematically avoid the Holy Communion. At other times, participation in the Holy Communion may bring into focus serious problems of the participant, so that he seeks out the pastor for help. We have known many persons whose emotional problems blocked any vital experience in worship, but in whom worship became a vital and living experience after they had found the resolution of their problem through a counseling relationship with the pastor. The counseling experience, essentially one of confession, can become a sacrament even though it may not be officially and theologically recognized as such.

Throughout this book we have been interpreting the sacramental nature of human relationships when they are lived within the context of the Gospel. It is essential to perform the sacramental rites which grow out of, and remind the worshiper of, experiences in the life of Jesus. But Jesus himself found in human relationships, and also in natural processes and events, meanings which communicated some truth about the Kingdom of God. And to Jesus, words themselves had a sacramental value—"the words that I have spoken to you are spirit and life" (John 6:63). Human relationships and the words which formulate and convey their meaning can communicate the deep realities of the Christian faith when these realities are present in experience, and only then. At such times relationships become sacramental. A cup of cold water given in genuine concern and respect for the recipient—that is, given in the spirit of Christ—portrays something of the grace of God. Genuine pastoral care is a constantly sacramental relationship.

Speaking and Hearing as One Process

So much of the work of the pastor involves verbal communication that some further technical comments on speaking and hearing are in order. The ear is a receptive organ. Hearing means taking in words, ideas, feelings, and making some response to them. Words may be accepted and remembered without a grasp of the meaning the words convey. One sees this in the student who has memorized theological or psychological words and can repeat them in speech or in writing, but who becomes confused and lost when asked to state what they mean or to use them meaningfully. It is possible to hear and accept an idea in verbal form while remaining unaware of or rejecting the content. We really understand a communication only to the extent that we are emotionally ready to grasp it. We hear what we want to hear, and often we do not hear the real communication. Perception of the outside world, either through seeing or hearing, follows patterns of the personality. This is especially true of the perception of relationships. Our perceptions are distorted by our own needs and defenses. Jesus understood that many had ears but could not hear in the deeper sense.

A great deal of hearing is negative. We have to say "No" before we can say "Yes," like the man in the parable of Jesus (Matt. 21:28-31). Our defenses are constantly operating, even though we are not aware of it. Indeed, we so identify our real self with our defensive processes that we spring to the defense of our defenses. Thus a student in a class in theology or psychology may reject an idea because it creates anxiety in him. Instead of examining his anxiety, he springs to the defense of his denial by becoming hostile to the teacher who presented the idea. Later when his anxiety subsides, he may wonder why he reacted so violently against the teacher, since he now hears the same idea in an altogether different way.

The process of identification is important in the speaker-hearer relationship—in the effectiveness of speaking and in the accuracy of hearing. Unless the person feels that the pastor is with him deeply, he will feel that what the pastor says is beside the point. How many times one hears a person say, "He just doesn't understand me," or "He doesn't know what I am going through," or "He is not concerned with me, but only with his own ideas." The speaker, being the one who has taken the initiative, will demonstrate his understanding or lack of understanding of his hearer. The hearer is very likely to respond in kind whether positively or negatively. (Or at least try to.) People need to feel understood, and then they tend to identify consciously or unconsciously with the speaker. A student may identify with a teacher because he sees something in the teacher that is like one of his parents. Such identification may be either positive or negative, but the "hearing" of the student will be affected by these conditions.[9] Likewise, individuals in a congregation may reject the message because they cannot accept the messenger. Or they may reject the messenger because they cannot hear and understand the message. In all forms of pastoral care the pastor and the kind of relationship he actually creates with others is a controlling factor.

Hearing is also affected by the fact that the spoken word may "cue off," or stimulate responses within the hearer. Sometimes it is not the word itself, but the tone of voice or inflection with which it is spoken. The same word spoken maliciously or in jest or seriously will cue off different responses. These responses are also related to the individual's previous experiences and their meanings. Thus the response of a person to the phrase "God is our heavenly father" may be either negative or positive, depending on his feelings about his earthly father and how he has handled these feelings, and also depending on the nature of his fantasies about heaven. Many words used in religious speech can cue off association in human relationships. Meanings developed in human relationships in early childhood may be associated with religious expressions in adult life, either positively or negatively. A person may find it impossible to accept or even to understand certain religious ideas because these ideas set off negative feelings based on his previous experiences. One student in a certain course found himself going to sleep when certain ideas which created intense hostility in him were expressed. He literally put himself out of hearing. Another student exposed to the same ideas will react with excitement and want to plunge into a heated discussion. The same words and ideas produce quite different responses because of the way in which they are heard, and this in turn is determined by meanings growing out of previous experiences. There is a great difference between that kind of religious education which teaches religious words and ideas, and the kind which aims at helping persons to understand the meaning of their relationships with man and God and to find appropriate words in which to formulate and communicate their ideas. The basis for a real community of spirit is not only the use of words in common, but more deeply the experience of common meanings.[10]

In the light of what we have been saying, we should look again at the insistence often heard today that "faith comes from what is heard, and what is heard comes by the preaching of Christ" (Rom. 10:17). There is certainly a literal truth in this statement. In the light of our discussion, two comments are in order. First, the preaching of Christ by a person who is anxious and guilt-laden, or who confuses faith with sentimental dependence and submissiveness, or who confuses Christ with creedal statements about Christ, will hardly produce a vital faith. Only the preacher whose own faith is genuine, and who is able to meet his people in self-giving love, will be able to preach in the manner which inspires living faith. Second, the hearers either must have experienced previously or feel at the moment of hearing, something of the reality in relationships for which Christ stands. It is not only the intellectual content of the sermon which is crucial, but the relationship which exists between speaker and hearer as well. There needs to be a measure of unity between this content and the quality of relationship. The statement of Paul is often interpreted in a mechanical manner which misses these deeper aspects of communication of the Gospel. So much preaching does not inspire faith because words and reality are not one, and Christ is not preached authentically.

So much has been written about the pastor as a listener that more may seem superfluous. However, the pastor will not be able to speak to the depths of another person until he has learned to listen to his own deeper feelings and meanings. He must listen below the level of the manifest content of speech. Also, the pastor will not be able to listen to others more deeply than he has listened to himself. It is in listening to himself and others that he may hear what Thurneysen repeatedly calls "the Word of God." This phrase as I use it here does not stand for some preformulated idea, but rather the reality of the man-to-man and man-to-God relationship as it is revealed in the crux of experience. Even while he is preaching, the pastor must learn to observe the responses of the congregation—according to facial expression, restlessness or attentiveness, the manner in which the congregation is listening. Such sensitivity can make it possible for him to respond in terms of their needs as these are being communicated at the moment, often unconsciously. Dependence on a written manuscript or on too full outline can seriously interfere with this dynamic process in preaching. Speaking and hearing is a total process in which the relationship of speaker and hearer is deeply involved.

Speaking and hearing, then, are really one process. As one hears, one speaks. Speech reveals the speaker, and sometimes discloses profound defensiveness, concealment, and lack of insight. In extreme form, speech can become psychotic delusion or hallucination. Or speech may grow out of a profound openness to oneself and the meanings of one's experiences, and then it becomes sharing. Such speech does not aim at manipulating; it aims at self-giving. But one cannot give until one discovers what it is one has to give. To be able to verbalize the meanings of one's experience is to have first received those meanings into consciousness, to become aware of them, to know oneself directly rather than to know about oneself. Speech that carries insight born of self-discovery has the possibility of communicating insight to others who are able to hear. Becoming a pastor is a matter of growth, of being and becoming, of openness to self and to others, rather than of learning the right verbal formula or how to say the correct thing. The frequent question of pastors, What do you say to persons in such-and-such a situation? should be changed to, What can I be to persons in such a situation?

Personal Obstacles to the Pastoral Relationship

We need to look at the pastor's personal obstacles to nonverbal, deeply personal communication in any aspect of the pastoral ministry. Such involvement with persons is actually very difficult for many pastors because of the nature of their own human relationships in the periods of growth from infancy to adulthood. Pastors are not of a different breed from other people, but possess the same needs, partake of the same kind of experience, and have the same kind of problems. In childhood a pastor may have been hurt by someone who loved him, or he may have been rebuffed when he endeavored to give love to others. If so, he may experience anxiety and perhaps guilt when he attempts to give love to his parishioners. Because he has been hurt he may have built defensive barriers around himself to keep people at arm's length, dealing with them intellectually but not relating to them as persons, observing their sufferings from an aloof position but not participating or sharing in their sufferings in any deep sense. Many pastors with this unconscious attitude find encouragement in their theological training—if they have the "right" theology, can speak the right formulas, and quote the right authorities, then they feel they can discharge their responsibilities. Our theological schools, which now place heavy and justifiable emphasis on intellectual training, should also accept their responsibility for helping men to become pastors in a deeper sense by creating opportunities for emotional and spiritual growth comparable to the intellectual training. But many pastors, because of a feeling of incompetence in the deeper levels of human relationships, react negatively to the idea that they can communicate the reality of the Gospel only by participating in the deepest sufferings of others in self-giving love. For in not having received at the point of their own deep needs, they have not learned to give. Or they may confuse superficial and sentimental acceptance of the idea with the authentic experience. When one hears a student or a pastor say, "All I have to do is to love people," he knows he is in the presence of one who is willing to accept the idea verbally as long as he does not have to take responsibility for inquiring what this means for him personally. Such pastors are not to be condemned: they need a rich experience of pastoral care, and in some cases deep psychotherapy, before they will be able to give a genuine love. Until this occurs they will not be able to participate in the sufferings of others. This is one reason why some pastors espouse the theory which says that all the preacher has to do is to "proclaim the Word" and leave the rest to God—a very comfortable doctrine for those who are threatened by personal involvement. The Word indeed needs to be proclaimed, but its deeper content can be communicated only by one who is deeply involved both in the Word and in the predicament of human beings.

There is another reason why communication in depth is difficult for many to understand. We have participated in a culture which tends to ignore if not deny the inner meaning of human relationships, and to stress utilitarian rather than personal values. We manipulate persons as things, and use them for our own ends. This culture is dominated by utilitarian, money-making patterns, in which persons are valued according to what they produce rather than as persons. Such a culture creates individuals who find it very difficult to understand and accept the personal values implicit in an incarnational religion.

Another cultural situation operates against understanding on the personal level. Our culture is dominated by science, and science deals with a level of reality which can be described effectively by means of verbal symbols. The truth of science is not affected by the personal attitudes of the communicator. But the pastor is communicating an order of reality entirely different from that of the scientist. To describe and communicate facts about objects or observable or measurable processes is quite different from communicating our personal meanings in relation to other persons, or to God. It is for this reason that many scientists have rejected religious truth or reality; they are so committed to their own plane of comprehension and method of communication that they reject other levels of reality and their appropriate language. The temptation of the pastor has been in the other direction: to seek to compete with science by developing his religious ideas into almost a "scientific system" to be communicated verbally. But the very nature of religious reality makes such exact verbal formulation impossible.

Still another reason why the idea of communication through

relationships is hard for some to understand is our tendency to overintellectualize emotional and spiritual problems. By this we mean the attempt to formulate our emotional and spiritual problems in intellectual terms, then to formulate an answer which is usually the reverse statement of the problem (e.g., the answer to fear is faith), and then to seek to "apply" the answer to themselves. This leads to the repression of dynamic aspects of the self, and thus to unhealthy results. Sometimes the counselor discovers the extent to which an individual has confined himself to a rigid intellectual system, but most of all repressing the deep emotional elements which created the problem he is trying to solve. For example, adherence to a rigid intellectual system and its promugation may be an attempt to solve the problem of insecurity. The problem is only concealed by a false sense of security accompanied by a compulsive need to justify oneself by convincing others of the truth of the system. Feelings of insecurity can be adequately dealt with only by working them through at their roots. The tendency to overintellectualize becomes extreme in some persons suffering from a schizophrenic illness, but most of us have sufficient inner conflict to find this false solution appealing. This tendency is very strong in modern culture and in the modern Church. If we only have the right formulations we can solve all problems, so we feel. For the pastor, this may mean having the "right theology" without sufficient regard for the deeper dimensions of "personhood" or Christian experience. Philip Watson,[11] in his book *The Concept of Grace,* points out that the sacraments of the Church stand guard against the overintellectualization of the Gospel. Many persons need the kind of relationship with a pastor which enables them to penetrate beneath their overintellectualizations. They fail to respond to the sacraments for the same reason that they need to overintellectualize: they cannot allow another person, human or divine, to get through to a part of themselves that they feel compelled to exclude even from their own consciousness. It is very painful if another touches a part of us we cannot accept in ourselves.

Pastoral Care and Judgment

Our interpretation of pastoral care may seem to leave open the question of judgment. We can say frankly that we see no place in pastoral care for the passing of judgment in terms of condemnation or name-calling, or of moralistic preachments. Judgment is the prerogative of God, not of man, and the pastor who easily assumes the responsibility of speaking for God in a condemnatory manner had better look into his own motives. We should understand that as we judge, so are we judged.

On the other hand, the need for judgment, in another meaning of the word, is inherent in life. As persons we are constantly in need of a sense of where we are, what we are, who we are, and where we are going. At times we need to face or be faced with the significance and consequences of our attitudes and actions. Every serious student of human life knows that each person has within himself forces and patterns which are destructive and those which are creative. Part of what it means to be human is that a person may become aware of, and exercise some direction of, these forces within himself. We do not experience this kind of awareness of the meaning of our own life by drawing into ourselves. We find it by evaluating or understanding ourselves in the light of another person with whom we are in a redemptive relationship. At times another person may need to speak the word which brings us to our senses, which breaks through our blind spots. But this word must be spoken in love, not in condemnation. A genuinely loving person can be angry and at the same time understanding. As a pastor, there may be times when I am angry at something destructive that I see a person doing to himself or to others, but I must speak to the person through love, and even then failure may result.

All of us at times need the experience of self-evaluation in the light of another person with whom we are in a redemptive relationship. At the moment of judgment, when one becomes aware of his guilt, he needs also to become aware of the reality of God's forgiveness, and of the alternatives of accepting or rejecting this forgiveness. When we reject the love offered by another we are not judging him; we are really judging ourselves as unworthy of that love or incapable of accepting it. Any feeling of guilt or sense of worthlessness is an act of self-judgment, but always in the light of an image of what we should be or desire to be. At times this image comes from others. However, the deepest guilt we can experience is the consciousness that we have not found our essential self. Out of our own guilt we may hurt others in order to bring punishment on ourselves or to justify self-punishment; but there is no redemption in this. The real need is to discover the truth about ourselves, which can happen only in relation to another who accepts us as we are, both guilty and forgiven.

The Christian understanding is that judgment belongs to God, not to man, that God does not pronounce judgment for its own sake, but that it serves the purpose of His redemptive love. This judgment is not spoken primarily in words, but in the consequences of our being what we are, the consequences of our feelings, attitudes, actions. Because we have often refused to accept the principle of psychological determinism, we have blinded ourselves to the fundamental cause-and-effect relationship that God has written into human life, while at the same time we exercise moralistic judgments which are often false and inadequate because they are based on externals. The task of the pastor is very frequently that of helping a person read the judgment that God is writing of his daily experience and being, in the very consequences of his acts and relationships. It is easy to thunder from the pulpit that whatsoever a man soweth that shall he also reap, but it is quite another thing to help a person come to understand the significance of this in his own being. Judgment is part of the communication of the Gospel, but it is the judgment of God, not of the pastor, and the task of the pastor is to mediate this judgment by helping the person discover what is happening to him in his own experience. And this process will proceed from person to pastor, not in the reverse, as the pastor meets the person in redemptive love. This is part of what it means to communicate the Gospel to persons at the point of their need; to help them discover their need, and simultaneously to bring them a relationship through which they can move to find the answer. Pastoral care is helping persons see all sides of their existence and its meaning, their potential for creative as well as destructive forms of being and becoming, and enabling them to choose in the light of the consequences. The will of God is not to be known so much through mystical intuition as through the consequences of our daily choices.

One other aspect of judgment should be mentioned here. The pastor stands under the same judgment as do the persons to whom he is attempting to communicate the Gospel. There is the demand that he take the beam out of his own eye so he may see more clearly to take the mote out of his brother's eye. A pastor's best insights into others will come through his insights into himself; it is this acceptance of his true humanity which should keep him genuinely humble. His own struggles and problems should lead him to resources which will be of great value in helping others.

Every person, including the pastor, stands in need of discovering the reality of his own being and the meaning of his own existence. This reality has both its creative and its destructive aspects. To be confronted with negative aspects of oneself without at the same moment becoming aware of creative resources is a seriously traumatic experience. The true pastor is one who has found the reality of his own being before God, who is aware of the destructive possibilities within his own nature, and who has brought these under some measure of subjection to the creative forces of his being through the grace of God. He is therefore a man of deep hope and courage, and faces others in hope and courage. Thus his love, reverence, and trust of others calls from them the potentials of their being. This is the matrix of the authority of the pastor as it was of Jesus'. People knew they were in the presence of a true human being when they faced him because his relationship with them carried its own authenticity and validity. In this way he mediated the love of God to them, and also a sense of what it means to be a true human being. The creeds tried to express this by the phrase "very God of very God and very man of very man." The true authority of the pastor rests on the same basis. His genuineness finds its own self-validation in the lives of those to whom he ministers. This will be his only authority in helping them to discover the reality of their own being, and to judge themselves in the light of the Person of Christ. The redemptive love of which we speak is the affirmation of the other as a person and as a child of God, a deep intention to help the other find the fulfillment of the potential which God has created in him, and the willingness to meet the other at the point of his deepest need, which will mean in his suffering.

Such communication of the Gospel through a relationship of love is described by Brunner[12] in the following words:

> In love I will the other person to be as he is, that is as God gives him to be, and yet at the same time I will him to be different, as God wishes him to be. But since, before all else, God wills that I should be different, since before all else, I must remember that by nature I oppose my will to that of the other, the first and also the surest sign of genuine love is my acceptance of the other person, the attitude which does not correct him, or "pull him up" or demand or resist. The distinctive mark of the Christian ethos . . . is positive love, self-sacrificing surrender, which from the psychological point of view is the highest activity.

Judgment needs to be related to acceptance. Acceptance involves and includes judgment. Acceptance is a relationship freely offered to another because he is a person, and because the giver is able to respect him as a person. Judgment is a necessary evaluation of the behavior of the person. It is the acceptance of facts about the person. If a man is a murderer, he should be accepted as a person who has committed a murder. Acceptance does not mean blinking at facts or realities; there is no cure or salvation in this. Cure or salvation will come only in an accepting relationship in which self-judgment and evaluation are encouraged through the pastor's ability to know the worst there is to know and still accept the other as a person deserving of understanding. In rare instances this understanding may be communicated in anger (Matt. 21:12; 23:1-36).

On the other hand, to demand acceptance from others is an expression of narcissism. Some persons demand the privilege of doing as they please regardless of the rights or needs of others, or without any legitimate social control, and of still being, in their own words, "accepted." But they are not really asking for acceptance; they are asking for indulgence. They want others—God, and the world—to be an indulgent parent while they are permitted to play the role of the infant. Acceptance in social relationships, or in a community, involves the rights and needs of others, and persons who demand indulgence deny these rights and needs. In a pastoral relationship the pastor must be prepared for demands for indulgence. If they are tolerated here—and sometimes they are—it is for the purpose of helping the person gain insight and make necessary changes in his behavior.

Sometimes, instead of demanding acceptance, a person will demand judgment from the pastor. In these instances he may be expressing a need to be punished or a need to be deeply dependent. These needs are both childish and unhealthy, and for the pastor to fall into the trap presented by such persons is to do them harm. But acceptance of these persons does not mean that he has to fall into this trap. It means that he accepts them as persons, but as persons who have particular needs, and where possible he seeks to help them understand and work through these tendencies. Again, there is a kind of judgment here, not in the sense of condemnation but in the sense of evaluation and helping another to make self-evaluation. Acceptance does not mean that we are to treat all others as they want us to treat them; to do this to some persons would be to reinforce their position and to encourage them to continue in some neurotic pattern—in short, to hurt them.

In describing the task of the pastor as the mediation of the love of God we are obviously stressing the central characteristic of God as seen in the Christian revelation, the Fatherhood of God. God as Father not only creates and sustains man, but seeks his redemption and fulfillment. But there is another aspect of the nature of God which is related to growth and to judgment, and that is the Lordship of God in Christ. The Lordship of God may be interpreted childishly in terms of an authoritarian, punishing attitude, or in terms of a more mature acceptance of responsibility for oneself before a God who is acknowledged as the ultimate authority in personal life. Tillich[18] has pointed out that the Lordship and Fatherhood of God need to be kept in constant tension in order to avoid making God into either a demonic power or a sentimental old man. The tendency to overremphasize one of these qualities in God at the expense of the other is not of a logical origin; it is rooted in a personal need for punishment or in a childish dependence and need for protection. Either bias leads to a neurotic kind of person and religion. On the other hand, a dynamic tension may be hard to maintain. This requires a certain level of emotional maturity. In the final analysis the pastor's own sense of the Lordship of Christ, or of the ultimate authority of God in the choices and decisions of daily life, will be communicated to those to whom he ministers. It is important that the pastor understand through his own experience that the Lordship of Christ is a necessary accompaniment of the redeeming love of God. In all human experience there is nothing so inexorable and demanding as love, and nothing that brings suffering into human life as does the lack of love. Christ could not have revealed the redeeming love of God without at the same time revealing the Lordship of God.

ᙡ 5 ᙡ

Pastoral Care and the Growth
of Persons

IN a previous chapter we referred to the traditional aproach in
pastoral care, that is, to the work of the pastor in dealing
with the natural crises of life. Discussions of pastoral care
have centered on such events as birth, marriage, illness, death.[1]
This approach has had certain values, not the least of which is
that at times of intense suffering from events in our common
experience some persons are more open to a pastoral ministry
than at other times.

But this approach also has its limitations. As we have indicated
earlier, the way in which a person meets one of these universal
crises is closely related to the level of emotional growth he has
achieved at the time, since the meaning of an event is determined quite as much, if not more, upon what a person brings to
it, as upon the event itself. Furthermore, many crises are produced by the failure of persons to grow emotionally.[2]

The idea of growth is not foreign to the Christian faith. Such
concepts as "growth in grace," and "going on to perfection" are
ample indication of this. But the Christian faith has not produced a workable theory of personal growth. This is not said in
criticism, but rather in delineation of a task; for such a theory of
growth is a psychological, not a theological, problem, although it
has many theological implications. Throughout the history of
pastoral care, current psychological theories have been utilized
by pastors in their work.[3] This is one indication that some such
theory is a necessary background for vital involvement with persons, which otherwise might deteriorate into a relationship controlled by the pastor's own prejudicies and fantasies.

Creative pastoral involvement, then, requires some understanding of what is going on within the person, that is, the processes by which he has become the person he is. However, the conceptual formulation of such processes must always be hypothetical, subject to revision and reformulation, and never considered as "ultimate truth."

Much of the criticism that the pastoral care movement is too much involved with Freudian theories has been the result of misunderstanding.[4] Some of these criticisms, however, have been based on a sound insight that might be stated thus: How can an adequate theory of pastoral care and its involvement with persons utilize a psychology which stresses the development and control of instinctual drives? Actually some advocates of the Freudian point of view in pastoral care have wrestled with this problem much more than have the critics, for they have been in a position to be conscious of its significance. But in so far as they were also familiar with the Biblical account of man, they have understood that many of the Freudian concepts, particularly Eros and Thanatos, are amply illustrated in Biblical material, always with an additional religious dimension.[5]

Any pastoral or religious understanding of man must give full consideration to the problem of man's instinctive drives as these are expressed in his daily experience, as well as to the problem of cultural opportunities and deprivations in the satisfaction of these drives. The Christian faith has sought to play a vital role in the "internalization" of the external authority of the culture through what Freud, called "the superego"; the Ten Commandments are an excellent example of this. However, the Christian faith has also been interested in the soul of man. In recent decades the word "soul" has suffered from misuse, and the word "self" has tended to replace it. Christian thinkers, however, have recognized an aspect of man which is not adequately formulated in the concepts of either instinctive drives or superego. Theologically speaking, this aspect is the soul or spirit; psychologically, it is the self or the ego.

Some Freudian analysts also have become aware of a dimension in persons that was not sufficiently elaborated in Freud's theory, and they have set about correcting this weakness. We refer to the development of ego psychology[6] in recent psychoanalytic thought. The work of Erik Erikson[7] on ego development is of particular significance for pastoral care. Erikson, a psychoanalyst and a specialist in child therapy, has also approached the problem of growth from the point of view of cultural anthropology. He is concerned not only with what is going on within the individual, but also with what the individual means to his culture and his culture means to him, and what these meanings may contribute to the process of ego development. Because of our conviction of the value of Erikson's approach for pastoral care, we shall outline his basic concepts. It should be kept in mind, however, that this discussion is not much more than an outline, the purpose of which is to encourage the reader to wrestle with Erikson's own works. We are not presenting his ideas as "ultimate truth," which indeed he would not do either, but rather as a stimulating and fruitful approach to some of the problems of ego development which are vital to pastoral care.

Here we need to speak frankly of two dangers to be avoided in considering Erikson's work. One is the tendency to try to turn new ideas into a program. Pastors who have not been adequately trained in pastoral care, or who may have personal problems which lead them to emphasize programs rather than personal relationships, or who have been overencouraged to organized activities by superiors, often overemphasize programs and the programming of ideas. Nothing could be further from the spirit of Erikson's work or from the essence of pastoral care! Repeatedly we will be saying that the basis for ego development is in human relationships, not in programs. Programs may furnish an opportunity for relationships and the communication of meanings through relationships, but programs in themselves may be used as a deadly substitute for deeper realities.

The other danger is the conversion of concepts of ego development into "oughts," that is, into ethical imperatives to be preached or a rigid system to be promulgated. To be sure, there is something of an ethical imperative implied in personality development itself. The person must grow, in ego, in conscience, and in impulses, or he becomes sick. But growth takes place through personal relationships, not through ethical preachments or legal systems. For example, Erikson[8] speaks of infancy as the stage in which the basic conflict is between trust and mistrust.

Trust in infancy may become the foundation for all trusting relationships throughout life, and we would add, for religious faith. Preachers are always looking for ways of reinforcing their insistence that persons have faith; but we need to see that faith, like trust in infancy, is not the product of exhortation or of being told that one should trust. Real trust grows out of relationships with a person or persons who are trustworthy and who show it in their daily contacts. So it is with all the other qualities of ego growth. The task of the pastor is not to tell persons how they ought to grow, but rather to help them by creating conditions and relationships within the Church which makes growth possible. Therefore, our purpose here is to increase the understanding of the pastor in his relationships, rather than to assist him directly in programming or preaching. But the pastor can be very sure that when he talks about faith in the pulpit his own trust or lack of trust will be felt by the congregation!

As a background to understanding Erikson, it is desirable to have a familiarity with the general theory developed by Freud: the concepts of the id, ego, and superego; the problem of anxiety, repression, and ego defenses; and the psychosexual stages of development. This approach is discussed helpfully in other works to which the reader is referred.[9]

The work of Erikson centers on understanding the ego and its development. The ego may be pictured as midway between the id and the superego. The word "ego" stands for those processes within the person which have the constant task of synthesizing inner needs and conflicts with the demands, frustrations, and values presented by other persons and the prevailing culture. In infancy, the ego processes are just beginning to develop, and may be very weak in relation to frustrations imposed by the environment, such as the withdrawal of love for whatever reason. Therefore, the ego may be subjected to problems of synthesis or integration for which it does not have the necessary strength. But it does have at its disposal certain "ego defenses,"[10] that is, psychological processes by which it can allay its anxiety and find substitute ways for the gratification of its needs. An ego defense is a substitute way of coping with a problem that cannot be directly mastered. One such defense is fantasy.

The ego has at its disposal in its synthesizing efforts the normal processes of perception, memory, imagination, reason, and motility. Defense mechanisms distort these normal processes in various ways. Says Erikson, "The ego, then, is an 'inner institution' evolved to safeguard that order within individuals on which all outer order depends. It is not 'the individual,' nor his individuality, although it is indispensable to it."[11] While the superego is the internal process by which the prohibitions and demands of the culture operate within the psyche, the ego reflects the personal meaning that the individual experiences in relation to those about him. In different ways, then, both the superego and the ego represent internal processes through which the culture and its values become part of a person.

Emphasis should be placed on the word "processes." Psychological terms such as ego and superego are constructs—a kind of shorthand language for the way in which constellations of dynamic processes are organized for purposes of thought and communication. Thus when we speak of "the ego" we do not have in mind a definite locale in the psyche, nor an objective "thing." We do have in mind constellations of processes which become organized into a psychic structure through which the functioning of the person is carried out—in the psychic realm, as in the organic, structure and function are but different aspects of life processes.

The process of developing an identity begins in infancy and continues throughout life (it is the crucial problem of adolescence). Says Erikson,

The growing child must derive a vitalizing sense of reality from the awareness that his individual way of mastering experience (his ego synthesis) is a successful variant of a group identity and is in accord with its space-time and life plan. . . . The conscious feeling of having a *personal identity* is based on two simultaneous observations: the immediate perception of one's selfsameness and continuity in time; and the simultaneous perception of the fact that others recognize one's sameness and continuity. . . . ego identity concerns more than the mere fact of existence, as conveyed by personal identity; it is the ego quality of this existence.[12]

Identity, then, is related to the synthesizing functions of the ego. But it is also related to the values and meanings of the group. It thus becomes a focal point for a vital expression of the person's relationship to his culture. The simultaneous perceptions involved in identity—recognizing one's own selfsameness and continuity in time and realizing that others recognize in him these same qualities—speaks of the relationship which the individual has with others in his culture. A sense of identity arises out of perception of common meanings—within the self and within the culture. Lack of identity means conflict—the person does not value himself as he perceives his culture valuing him or disvaluing him. There is a sense then in which the ego and its identity are the individual's sense of his own value to himself and to others, his acceptance or nonacceptance, his being good or evil. Says Erikson, "the young individual must learn to be most himself where he means most to others—those others, to be sure, who have come to mean most to him. The term identity expresses such a mutual relation in that it connotes both a persistent sameness within oneself (selfsameness) and a persistent sharing of some kind of essential character with others."[13]

The sense of identity is related to the mechanism of identification. Through identification, children take into themselves characteristics of persons who influence them strongly either positively or negatively. But these separate identifications offer no unity; indeed they can become the basis of conflict when the child tries to pattern himself after conflicting identifications. We have known, for example, a young man whose vocational identifications with different persons led him both toward the ministry and toward medicine. He finally tried to solve his problem by becoming a hospital chaplain! But this was a projection of a fantasy, and not a real identity, since at the time he made his decision he had no real idea of what a hospital chaplain was. A sense of identity is formed as the individual sorts out his childhood identifications, retaining some, rejecting others, but in the final decision, putting the stamp of his own individuality on, and making his own unique organization of, the outcome, which is his own identity. As Erikson points out, society *identifies the young individual,* recognizing him as somebody who had to become the way he is, and who, being the way he is, is taken for granted."[14] He goes on to say that in forming an identity, the individual asks for recognition by the community, which the community is very happy to give; but it may react with hostility if the offer is rejected. The classical illustration of this is the persecution of

heretics by the Church! Identity is in part the gift of the group—
a cultural process communicated through relationships. This is at
least a part of the psychological meaning of the rituals of
baptism and confirmation.

A person's identity—or his failure to find an identity, and
therefore his lostness—is rooted in his historical-cultural tradi-
tions. The illness of the individual may reflect the illness of the
culture, and may in turn be reflected in the culture. Erikson[15]
has three works on this theme of the relation of the individual
ego and history. His study of Luther not only reveals the conflict
of the culture within the man Luther, but also the manner in
which historical-cultural change and individual pathology is tied
up with theological and religious ideas and practices. In this
scrutiny, religion does not always emerge on the side of goodness!

This brings us to a problem as deep in human experience as it
is in the Christian faith. In forming a sense of identity the individual has to sort out the evil from the good, and hopefully
discard the evil. However experience has proved that this is no
simple matter. Society and the Church usually hold the individual responsible for this selection, not recognizing that in many
and subtle ways society or the group itself has had a powerful
hand in the selection. The struggle between good and evil is a
problem for every human being, but in the emotionally sick
person it becomes intensified. As Erikson[16] indicates, there is an
unconscious evil identity—that which the ego is most afraid to
resemble. This identity is made up of images that have been
disturbing to the ego. The ego does not separate these memories
nor discriminate between them, but lumps them together as bad
or sinful under some symbol of evil.

Erikson[17] indicates that in our society the unconscious evil
identity is usually composed of images of: (1) the violated body
(a reference to the Freudian castration fear), (2) the ethnic out-
group, and (3) the exploited minority. This seems to explain
why ethnic outgroups and exploited minorities are often labeled
as sexual perverts of one kind or another—all three "evil" images
have become associated within the ego. He also points out the
"sad truth that in any system based on suppression, exclusion,
and exploitation, the suppressed, excluded, and exploited uncon-

sciously believe in the evil image which they are made to represent by those who are dominant."[18] In this regard he has some unusually poignant remarks on the identity of the American Negro which should be read by all concerned with the present racial struggle—and by those who are not yet concerned! It can be seen from this brief summary that Erikson has moved beyond the strictly individualistic approach of traditional psychoanalysis, although his work is rooted in that discipline. His concept of ego identity, in which the individual is related to the historical-cultural processes of which he is a part, presents many fruitful leads for the pastor or the interpreter of religion.

Erikson is as much, if not more, concerned with the growth of the healthy personality, as he is with pathological development. In his formulations of growth he uses the epigenetic principle of biology as an analogy. "Somewhat generalized, this principle states that anything that grows has a *ground plan,* and that out of this ground plan the *parts* arise, each part having its *time* of special ascendancy, until all parts have arisen to form a *functioning whole.*"[19] This means that personality is not entirely the result of its social environment: the growing person brings to experiences of social interaction potentialities of his own that emerge in a certain time-growth sequence, and "the healthy child, given a reasonable amount of guidance, can be trusted to obey inner laws of development, laws which create a *succession of potentialities for significant interaction* with those who tend him."[20] For example, the first ego potentiality in infancy is trust. If trust is not learned in infancy, it becomes more difficult or, under some circumstances, impossible to learn later in life. Furthermore, it becomes the basis on which positive ego qualities develop after infancy. But these qualities exist as undeveloped potentials before the stage in which they receive critical development. Thus the autonomy which characterizes second stage of ego growth is present in some undeveloped form in earlier infancy.

No ego quality, such as trust, emerges without crisis or conflict. Thus the child may and does experience in infancy relationships which create mistrust. Erikson speaks of this conflict as a "decisive encounter" with the social environment. Other persons communicate to the infant their particular feelings and meanings for him, and these are positive or negative, good or evil,

Thus "Each stage becomes a crisis because incipient growth and awareness in a significant part function goes together with a shift in instinctual energy and yet causes specific vulnerability in that part."[21] Shifts in instinctual energy are usually reflected in changes in behavior, interests, and goals. Thus in certain respects a child may have consolidated his strengths, while in others he may seem weak and uncertain. When this occurs he is especially vulnerable, and other persons react in various ways to his sense of weakness. It may be a signal for some to do too much for the child rather than encouraging him to do for himself. At least there will be a response, a fact which leads Erikson to write, "A family can bring up a baby only by being brought up by him. His growth consists of a series of challenges to them to serve his newly developing potentialities for social interaction."[22]

Thus each successive step in growth "is a potential crisis because of a radical *change in perspective.*"[23] But the crises of growth, when they become serious, are also crises in the relationships between the child and "significant others" when mutual regulation has broken down.

The concept of mutual regulation is in direct contrast with the principle of relationships which operates in many homes, that is, control of one another. It is not always the parent who controls the child; the child may control the parent. Erikson sees the needs of the child and his parents as complementary: the child needs a relationship of nurturing trust and autonomy, and the parent, if he is an emotionally healthy person, needs to give such nurture. Thus there is a reciprocity of need. When the individuals in a family are controlling themselves in a manner appropriate to age and status, mutual regulation results.

The patterns of mutual regulation change as the child grows and the parent matures. Such patterns cannot successfully be developed artificially or by precept, since they really consist of the subtle but powerful interactions of persons with each other and are often motivated below the level of consciousness. Any pattern of relationships that depends on exploitation, domination, or possessiveness destroys mutuality. What are usually taken as "behavior problems" in children may be symptomatic of a breakdown of mutuality between parent and child. It would seem then that energy spent in attempts to teach children the difference between good and evil would be used to better advantage in helping them to understand themselves in their relationships with others, particularly the ways in which their own attitudes and actions are destructive.

Basic Trust versus Basic Mistrust

The first crisis in ego development is characterized by Erikson as that of trust or mistrust. This occurs in the first year of life, when the capacity for trust emerges from within the child and seeks a response in the mother. In calling such attitudes "basic," Erikson means that they pervade both the surface and the depth of the personality, that is, they are part of conscious experience and ways of behaving, and are also unconscious inner states. He regards "basic trust as the cornerstone of a healthy personality."[24]

The impairment of basic trust in infancy is experienced as a sense of mistrust. Mistrust, which is a form of anxiety, makes it impossible for the individual to find comfortable relations with others or with self.

The crisis of trust or mistrust—the emergence of the need and its answer or frustration by those caring for the infant—is related to feeding in this "incorporative stage," when not only is the child receptive to food, but also to emotional satisfaction, comfort, and a sense of well being, that is, a sense of being given to as he needs. As Erikson[25] says, the infant "lives through and loves with his mouth; and the mother lives through, and loves with, her breasts." The attitudes of the mother toward herself as a woman and a mother, and toward her child, are important ingredients in her effort to provide emotional as well as physical nourishment. Here is an illustration of "mutual regulation" between the individual and another person. "The mutuality of relaxation thus developed is of prime importance for the first experience of friendly otherness: from psychoanalysis one receives the impression that in thus *getting what is given,* and in learning to *get somebody to do* for him what he wishes to have done, the baby also develops the necessary groundwork to get to be the giver, to 'identify' with her."[26] The sense of trust developed in this relationship becomes the basis for a sense of identity in the child, a feeling that he has meaning and worth both to himself and to others.

But frustration is inevitable, and Erikson sees the crisis coming during the second part of the first year, when there is an increase of physiological tension owing to teething and other changes, when the infant is able to distinguish himself from other objects and is becoming aware of himself as a person, and when the mother is likely to turn away from the infant in favor of other activities. There is a certain leeway in what may happen to a child in terms of frustration. Erikson is clear that it is not frustration in itself that is damaging, but the failure to communicate meaning to the child. "Parents must not only have certain ways of guiding by prohibition and permission; they must also be able to represent to the child a deep, an almost somatic conviction that there is a meaning to what they are doing."[27]

Out of the crisis of the oral stage, where experiences of trust or mistrust are crucial, arises a deep sense of loss. "Our clinical work indicates that this point in the individual's early history provides him with some sense of basic loss, leaving the general impression that once upon a time one's unity with a maternal matrix was destroyed."[28] This loss is usually related to weaning—perhaps breast feeding was abruptly withdrawn when the infant began biting—and to a general loss by the infant of the mother's attention and presence as other demands are made upon her time and energy. The sense of loss may be such as to create acute infantile depression or a mild, chronic state of mourning that can affect the rest of a person's life. "But even under more favorable circumstances, this stage seems to introduce into the psychic life a sense of division and a dim but universal nostalgia for a lost paradise. It is against the combination of these impressions of having been deprived, of having been divided, and of having been abandoned, all of which leave a residue of basic mistrust, that basic trust must be established and maintained."[29]

Obviously, no infant arrives at the end of the first year without some experiences which create mistrust, but it is to be hoped that he has had enough experiences which inspire trust to outweigh them. Erikson is clear on the need to establish enduring patterns for the balance of basic trust over mistrust. This is first of all a task for maternal care, and it "does not seem to depend on absolute *quantities of food or demonstrations of love,* but rather on the *quality* of the maternal relationship."[30]

Erikson describes trust using almost the same terms as for identity, indicating that trust is a fundamental ingredient in the sense of identity. "The general state of trust . . . implies not only that one has learned to rely on the sameness and continuity of the outer providers but also that one may trust oneself and the capacity of one's own organs to cope with urges; that one is able to consider oneself trustworthy enough so that the providers will not need to be on guard or to leave."[31] In words current in theological circles today, trust is essential to the development of a sense of community; the infant must experience a safe and satisfying relationship with others, through which he gains emotional strength to cope with problems presented to him both by his world and from within himself.

On the relation of trust to religion, Erikson has some significant comments. He is concerned with whether or not in any given group "religion and tradition are living psychological forces creating the kind of faith and conviction which permeates a parent's personality and thus reinforces the child's basic trust in the world's trustworthiness."[32] He draws analogies between much that religion promises and the context of infancy, such as the need to be provided for and to trust in a provider. Also, "All religions have in common . . . the insight that individual trust must become a common faith, individual mistrust a commonly formulated evil." He concludes: "Whosoever says he has religion must derive a faith from it which is transmitted to infants in the form of basic trust; whosoever claims that he does not need religion must derive such basic faith from elsewhere."[33] For an intensely stimulating and illuminating discussion of the conflict of trust and mistrust in a religious genius, the reader is referred to Erikson's *Young Man Luther.*

Autonomy or Shame and Doubt

The second crisis of ego development, beginning in the second year, centers on another organ and its functioning. In classical Freudian language, this is the anal stage. According to Erikson, the process of toilet training provides opportunities for mutual self-regulation which can have a far-reaching influence on the development of the ego. He sees the basic crisis here as between autonomy on the one hand and shame and doubt on the other.

The psychosocial modalities of this stage are retention and elimination—"holding on" and "letting go." Hoarding things or throwing things away is expressed not only in toilet training, but in many activities of the child. Indeed, if the adults co-operate he will make a game out of this with his toys which can perhaps be carried over to his toilet experiences. For the first time he is being asked to learn to control his muscular structure, and this requires learning an inner control. The child at this stage is often as "having a mind of its own," that is, he shows an emerging capacity for autonomy, for making the decision for retention or elimination, holding on or letting go.

Erikson sees this stage as a severe test for the mutual regulation between mother and child. If maternal control is too early or too rigid, it destroys the opportunity for the child to learn to control his functions and activities by his own free choice, and this leads to a sense of defeat and rebellion.

This stage, therefore, becomes decisive for the ratio between love and hate, for that between cooperation and willfulness, and for that between the freedom of self-expression and its suppression. From a sense of *self-control without loss of self-esteem* comes a lasting sense of autonomy and pride; from a sense of muscular and anal impotence, of loss of self-control, and of parental overcontrol comes a lasting sense of doubt and shame.[34]

The development of autonomy rests on a continuation of the earlier sense of trust. Out of such trust, combined with firm treatment, the child will sense that what is being asked of him has meaning for him, and he will feel some protection from his own strong urges.

The alternative to autonomy, a sense of inner decision in making one's movements, is shame and doubt, which reflect a sense of helpless exposure that one would like to escape, and a real question as to one's value as a person. What Erikson calls the modalities of "holding on" and "letting go" can find either positive or destructive expression toward society or toward the self. One negative result in the child is the development of the tendency to "overmanipulate himself," to develop a "precocious conscience." Such a person becomes the classical "compulsive" character—repetitive, stingy, needing to hold on rather than let go, and needing to control. Or he may become the kind of person who, failing in any genuine autonomy, puts on a show of autonomy in an overcompensatory way.

Erikson sums up his advice to parents of children at this stage: "be firm and tolerant with the child at this stage, and he will be firm and tolerant with himself. He will feel pride in being an autonomous person; he will grant autonomy to others; and now and again he will even let himself get away with something."[35] He warns that there is no substitute for genuine autonomy in the parents themselves, just as there is no substitute for their genuine trustworthiness. "When it comes to human values, nobody knows how to fabricate or manage the fabrication of the genuine article. . . . For no matter what we do in detail, the child will feel primarily what we live by, what makes us loving, cooperative, and firm beings, and what makes us hateful, anxious and divided in ourselves."[36] Erikson's stress on values as communicated through relationships, and on the corollary of this, that parents, teachers, and pastors cannot give what they do not have, is shared by many who are engaged in helping others.

Initiative versus Guilt

If the child has successfully resolved the conflict of autonomy versus shame and doubt which is characteristic of the second year of life, he will be ready to face the next ego crisis, that of initiative versus guilt. He has already shown the capacity to try to get what he wants; now, and in a special way, the impulse to be "self-activated" emerges as a dominant quality. Successful resolution of the previous conflicts becomes the basis for growth at this stage.

The stage of life from three to about six or seven is known in Freudian terms as the period of the Oedipus complex—the period in which the boy has feelings of a sexual nature toward his mother and a sense of resentment toward his father, who seems to stand in his way. Erikson's work incorporates all of the stages of psychosexual development described by Freud, but he moves beyond the vicissitudes of the instinctive drive to the problem of ego development associated with a given period of the child's life.

The child at this stage is able to move about; his energy and

curiosity propel and guide his movements. He is observant, inclined to ask questions endlessly, and he can understand in a
childish manner the patterns and roles of adults in his environment. Now he is able to play with other children, and they learn
from one another. "His learning now is eminently intrusive and
vigorous: it leads away from his own limitations and into future
possibilities."[37] The psychosocial mode of this stage then is intrusive, "intrusion into other bodies by physical attack; the intrusion into other people's ears and minds by aggressive talking;
the intrusion into space by vigorous locomotion; the intrusion
into the unknown by consuming curiosity."[38]

The sexual curiosity of this stage is focused on the sexual
organs and their possible uses. Sexual play of various kinds with
other children takes place. However, the wish of the child for
sexual relationship with the parent of the opposite sex, and at
the same time to take the place of the parent of the same sex,
becomes the source of much fantasy, hostility, and guilt. In many
ways the child is inadequate in comparison with the adult, but
here he is especially inadequate and subject to frustration. Consequently, a strong sense of guilt is likely to arise—"a strange
sense, for it forever seems to imply that the individual has committed crimes and deeds which, after all, were not only not committed but also would have been biologically quite impossible."[39]

It is at this stage that conscience, "the great governor of initiative," becomes firmly established. "The child now feels not only
ashamed when found out but also afraid of being found out. He
now hears, as it were, God's voice without seeing God."[40]

Conscience can be oversevere, cruel, and inhibiting, and can
burden the child with so much guilt in regard to his sexual and
hostile feelings that his initiative is blocked or seriously ham-
pered in its expression. For example, the child's curiosity, not
only about sexual matters but about all things, may be so seriously curtailed that he does not want to learn new things. The
sense of guilt is likely to make the child feel that he, rather than
his behavior, is bad, and he may look for ways to prove that he is
not. On the other hand, he may act badly in order to draw
punishment and thus alleviate his guilt for a time. Erikson
points out that one of the common forms of overcompensation

for the feeling of being bad or worthless in our culture is finding a sense of worth in what we are doing or are going to do, rather than in what we are, with the consequent overdevelopment of drive toward activities.

The answer to this phase is continued mutual regulation of the life of children and adults. Again, there is no substitute for giving the child genuine love and understanding, accepting his conflicts and problems, and doing things together with him in a way which helps him anticipate his someday becoming a competent adult—competent in love and work. Erikson points out that there is no time when the individual is more ready to learn quickly to become "big in the sense of sharing obligation, discipline, and performance rather than power, in the sense of *making things, instead of 'making' people,* than during this period of his development. He is also eager and able to *make things together.*"[41] A sense of equality in worth is expressed in the companionship of parent and child, particularly when they are of the same sex. The child's feeling of sharing rather than a sense of being exploited on the basis of weakness or size, will help him overcome his guilt, at least in a measure, and prevent it from becoming a crippling factor in his ego. He will retain initiative, guided by conscience, and by the values learned in the relationships he has experienced with his parents and other adults.

Industry and Inferiority

In the next period of growth, the classical "latency" period, no new drives emerge to be mastered. But it is a period of great social learning and ego development, and this is the aspect we are about to consider. Movement into the latency period, as with all periods, will not only mean that the child faces new tasks, but also that he will need to face and seek to resolve the emotional conflicts carried over from previous stages of growth. At this stage the child wants to learn how to do and make things both on his own and with others.

Now the child is sent to school, and he begins the process of learning in a formal setting—through prescribed duties or more adventurously, according to the system. But the child also likes to play, and it is important at this time, for the benefit of his later life, for him to learn to work when he works and play when he plays. Erikson points out, however, that play for the child is not recreation in the adult sense, but is often the child's "way of thinking over difficult experiences and of *restoring a sense of mastery.*" If the child's first play is properly handled by adults, "the *pleasure of mastering toy things* becomes associated with the *mastery of the conflicts* which were projected on them and with the *prestige* gained through such mastery." Since play at this age usually involves other children, and the child is introduced into a world of sharing with his peers, play now becomes a means of learning to master experience by "mediating, experimenting, planning, and sharing."[42]

The child at this stage wants to be useful, to be able to make things and to make them well. Erikson calls this the sense of industry. Skillful guidance at this stage is important; but if the child's conflicts in previous stages have not been sufficiently resolved, he may not want to grow to be competent in doing and making. He will be content to let others do and make for him. This can create a sense of inadequacy and inferiority—a danger at this stage—which may continue into adult life.

The child derives a sense of his social value through his meaning to others as someone who can do something worthwhile. When, however, doing or making things becomes a matter of competition with others or a way of defeating others, activity is in part motivated by hostile feelings, and no sense of mastery or industry will result. According to Erikson, this is "socially a most decisive stage: since industry involves doing things beside and with others, a first sense of *division of labor* and of *equality of opportunity* develops at this time."[43]

Identity versus Identity Diffusion

We have already dealt in a general way with the problem of ego identity. In adolescence achieving or maintaining a workable identity is the central problem. The sense of identity which has accrued up to this time may be disturbed because of new and quite radical physical growth and the emergence of sexual feelings and potentialities not hitherto experienced. At the same time society faces youth with problems of vocational commitment which are not unrelated to his sexual commitments. The task now before the adolescent is to re-form his sense of identity, to find a new sense of continuity and sameness which others can accept. In order to do this, he may again have to face unresolved crises of earlier periods.

As indicated earlier, ego identity is the integration of the identifications which the young person has previously made. But it is more than this, for he has brought to these identifications a selective process and also the stamp of his own individuality, so that the final synthesis is a unique identity.

The danger in adolescence is identity diffusion. Here the youth is unable to integrate his emerging forces with the positive or negative values of his childhood relationships and come to a sense of his meaning to his world. Erikson[44] comments that "it is primarily the inability to settle on an occupational identity which disturbs young people," and that the intolerance of many adolescents is a "necessary *defense against a sense of identity diffusion.*" However, there seems to be considerable identity conflict in youth today on the sexual level and also, as seen from within the pastoral ministry, on the religious level. The youth caught in a sense of identity diffusion not only cannot make decisions and move toward meaningful goals, but he also is at the mercy of his impulses as well as of his conscience. Erikson says that "a gradually accruing ego identity is the only safeguard against the *anarchy of drives* as well as the *autocracy of conscience,* that is, the cruel overconscientiousness which is the inner residue in the adult of his past inequality in regard to his parent."[45]

Another concept related to the identity crisis is that of the moratorium. This is society's way of providing, and the youth's way of accepting, situations in which identity decisions may be postponed. Erikson refers to Luther's early years in the monastery as such a moratorium.[46] Certainly anyone dealing with students today can observe them using college, and even seminary, as a way of postponing the decision as to what they are to be. The frequency with which some students change their major fields of study, or their inability to make a decision as to future vocation, is using the moratorium in an attempt to solve the problem of identity diffusion.

Another concept significant in relation to the adolescent is that of a negative identity, "meaning an identity which he has been warned *not* to become, which he can become only with a divided heart, but which he nevertheless finds himself compelled to become, protesting his wholeheartedness."[47] Parents often have a way of realistically presenting to the child the very patterns they consider dangerous and undesirable. Sometimes, in order to solve an identity crisis, the youth chooses a negative identity. "Many a late adolescent, if faced with continuing diffusion, would rather *be nobody or somebody bad, or indeed, dead—and this totally, and by free choice—than be not-quite-somebody.*"[48]

Much has been written about the "storm and stress" of adolescence. This period, says Erikson, "is not an affliction but a *normative crisis,* i.e., a normal phase of increased conflict characterized by a seeming fluctuation in ego strength, and yet also by a high growth potential. . . . What under prejudiced scrutiny may appear to be the onset of a neurosis is often but an aggravated crisis which might prove to be self-liquidating and, in fact, contributive to the process of identity formation."[49]

From a research project of a university health service comes material supporting Erikson's concept of identity conflict and diffusion. This is a study of "an acute confusional state in college students."[50] The authors consider this state to be "an emergency anxiety reaction to a combination of stressful conditions, where environmental insecurity is associated with internal conflicts of both shame and guilt in young adults of reasonably strong ego, who have suffered severe infantile trauma." The symptoms presented include (1) confusion, (2) inability to concentrate, (3) a feeling of helplessness, (4) a feeling of terrified isolation. With treatment the prognosis is good; without treatment it may be doubtful, and pathological conditions may result. The authors conclude:

In childhood these patients were bound in an extraordinarily strong dependent relationship to their parents through guilt and fear, engendered by parental instability and disharmony. With subsequent dependent gratification and support these patients were able to achieve a conforming type of adjustment and to gain success in academic and social achievements. However, in young adulthood when they attempted to find their own identity, through choice of heterosexual partner and choice of career, in the college environment, devoid of dependent gratification, their previous adjustment was inadequate to meet their needs. Sexual temptation or commitment may lead to guilt, which may lead to retreat. Retreat, in turn, may lead to shame and ridicule from the peer group. To avoid the shame, another attempt at conforming sexual behavior may be attempted, and once more guilt, retreat and shame. In this way, either thrusts toward accomplishment or retreat from it are associated with anxiety. Under these circumstances, if the dependent gratification from parents is cut off, due to their criticism or disapproval, the patient regresses to an early childhood fixation point, associated with primary anxiety, rage, and confusion, where he feels isolated, worthless, mistrustful and depressed. Recovery may occur when the patient, who desperately seeks help, finds someone to lean upon. If no one to meet his needs is found, reaction formation to the rage (the wish to save mankind rather than destroy it), introjection or projection may result.

Intimacy and Distantiation versus Self-Absorption

We come now to the first stage of adult life, where the ego, if it has successfully resolved the crises of the previous stages, is inwardly ready for intimacy. Erikson is clear that sexual intimacy is only part of what he has in mind. Indeed, persons who are confused in their identity may enter into sexual relationship without experiencing intimacy. He is, rather, speaking of an "interpersonal intimacy," which includes the sexual but also a close emotional and social relationship of a deeply satisfying and mutual nature. One basic condition for intimacy is a firm sense of identity—"the condition of a true twoness is that one must first become oneself."[51]

"The counterpart of intimacy is distantiation: the readiness to repudiate, to isolate, and, if necessary, to destroy those forces and people whose essence seems dangerous to one's own."[52] On the other hand, because of the fear of loss of identity, a youth may avoid any kind of interpersonal relationships, and move toward isolation and self-absorption. Distantiation, however, maintains contact with others, albeit a manipulative, exploitive contact; while isolation means withdrawal, and if developed to an extreme form, becomes schizophrenia.

Erikson's description of mature sexuality ("genitality" in psychoanalytic language) has meaning for the experience of intimacy. "The idea clearly is that the experience of the climactic mutality of orgasm provides a supreme example of the mutual regulation of complicated patterns and in some way appeases the potential rages caused by the daily evidence of the oppositeness of male and female, of fact and fancy, of love and hate, of work and play. Satisfactory sex relations make sex less obsessive and sadistic control superfluous."[53] Another way of saying this is that mutuality in sexual relations serves the purposes of emotional growth and well-being, but when mutuality is absent sex contributes to conflict and illness. But real mutuality in sex depends on a level of mutuality of being in which persons are open and self-revealing to each other in thoughts, feelings, and goals, and also in sexuality. The roots of many of the problems, and also of the joys, of marriage and family life will be found here.

Generativity versus Stagnation

In the next stage of adulthood Erikson calls generativity, "because it concerns the establishment (by way of genitality and genes) of the next generation."[54] It is primarily the interest in establishing and guiding the next generation. As such, generativity is a stage of growth of the healthy personality, and "where such enrichment fails altogether, regression from generativity to an obsessive need for pseudo intimacy takes place, often with a pervading sense of stagnation and interpersonal impoverishment."[55]

The mature person needs to be needed quite as much as the offspring needs to be cared for. But some persons find it difficult to develop a concern for the nurture and guidance of the younger generation; they may produce children, but find the care of children difficult or burdensome because of their own immaturity. Erikson finds the reasons for such failure "in early childhood impressions; in faulty identifications with parents; in excessive self-love based on a too strenuously self-made personality; and finally (and here we return to the beginnings) in the lack of some faith, some 'belief in the species,' which would make a child appear to be a welcome trust of the community."[56]

Integrity versus Despair and Disgust

The final stage of growth is that of later maturity characterized on the positive side by Erikson, as integrity, or "the acceptance of one's own and only life cycle and of the people who have become

significant to it as something that had to be and that, by necessity, permitted of no substitutions."[57] This includes the resolution of ambivalences in regard to, and a new acceptance of, one's
own parents; the acceptance of responsibility for one's own life; a
sense of fellowship with all other persons, now and through history, who have communicated human dignity and love. Ego integrity "is the ego's accrued assurance of its proclivity for order
and meaning. It is a post-narcissistic love of the human ego—not
the self—as an experience which conveys some world order and
spiritual sense, no matter how dearly paid for."[58]

One does not come to any final sense of ego integrity without
having won a large measure of the positive values in each of the
preceding stages of growth. On the other hand, failure to achieve
a wholesome sense of integrity in the final stage brings a sense of
despair and "an often unconscious fear of death: the one and
only life cycle is not accepted as the ultimate of life."[59] However,
time is short and it is impossible to start another life cycle in a
belated attempt to find integrity. Such despair often shows itself
as disgust with particular institutions or persons, a disgust which
disguises the individual's contempt for himself. "Ego integrity,
therefore, implies an emotional integration which permits participation by followership as well as acceptance of responsibility of
leadership."[60]

Comments and Questions

To develop all of the possible theological and pastoral implications of Erikson's thought is a task too large for the scope of
any one book. His theories are profound and comprehensive, and
are still developing.

Not all pastors will find the same meanings for their work in
his interpretations, and this is as it should be. His work is especially significant for the pastor because it places the inner world
of the individual in a dynamic relationship to his cultural environment and human relationships. In doing this Erikson does
not discard basic concepts of Freud, but he does elaborate the
processes of ego development more fully. Also he has been able to
see in the lives of his patients the meaning of their cultural
environment to them and, in turn, their meaning in relation to
their cultural environment. He is as concerned with the impact

of personality on culture as he is with the impact of culture on personality. These two relationships cannot be separated.

Much of the work of the pastor falls in this area of the relationship of personality and culture. Any pastoral perspective which overemphasizes either approach to the exclusion of the other will not be effective. The social-gospel approach of the past generation suffered from this limitation. Pastoral counseling is sometimes characterized as a purely individual approach, with no social consequences. But the pastoral counselor is aware of the impact of his work with one individual on a group of persons (a family), and of the impact of the group on one individual. And there is also a vocational perspective which is important for the pastor, and that is whether he sees himself as a teacher, a reformer, a preacher, or with some other function. In each of these he needs to define his goals in the light of personality-culture processes, if he wants to utilize the forces which mold persons. His theological orientation should contribute to this end. The goal for pastoral care, as we have been defining it in this book, is reconciliation, the resolution of conflict, the bringing together of the separated, the healing of both persons and society.

Erikson finds the answer to conflicts between individuals and between groups in the discovery of a more inclusive identity in which both sides may share and find a greater fulfillment. The pastor would understand the Christian faith as offering such an identity. It has been called variously the Kingdom of God, the brotherhood of man under the Fatherhood of God, and the Christian community. But the pastor must do more than preach these goals. He must learn new ways to participate as a pastor in the conflicts of individuals and of groups in a relationship which leads to reconciliation or healing. This takes the pastor directly into the life experiences of his people, especially those experiences which most powerfully affect their existence. There is no area of human conflict foreign to the work of the pastor. The creative processes of God are at work in all human relationships, and the pastor should become the catalyst to help to bring these forces to fruition.

The study of Erikson will bring home to the pastor a fact that he may have already gathered from other sources. We speak of the great importance of the first five or six years of life for the later development of the person. If the sense of basic trust, for example, is not developed in infancy, it may be exceedingly difficult if not impossible to develop later. If the pastor reflects on the meaning of the developmental process as outlined by Erikson, he should become aware of the tremendous importance of pastoral care of the infant, the child and its parents. If there is any one place where the emphasis of the church needs to be placed, it is with the parents of children under six years of age. This is not to minimize other stages of growth, but to stress the obvious fact that in infancy and early childhood significant beginnings in personal growth are made, or else they are not made. These beginnings center largely in the relationship of child and parent, in the feelings, values, and meanings they have for each other, and in how these are communicated. The relation of the parents to the larger group, and how that group evaluates parenthood and its responsibilities, is also important here. The problems of many adolescents and adults are basically the unresolved problems of early childhood, expressed in various distorted and symbolic ways. Growth needs to begin at the right time and the right place. Failure in growth at one stage makes the resolution of the crisis of the next stage very difficult. Basic ego qualities are best learned in their optimal stage.

Since it is necessary that any pastoral care of the small child be given through the parents, we should stress the value of nonverbal communication of feeling and meaning through relationships. Even the five- or six-year-old child may be struggling with feelings which are completely beyond his power to formulate in words—feelings of guilt, for example. Nor does he have to be told that he is forgiven or accepted. If the adults who are most significant to him really forgive and accept him, he will know it, and will not have to be told. In turn he will learn to be forgiving, even though he may not be able to verbalize it.

The fact that pastoral care of the child must be given through the parents deepens the responsibility of laymen in the world—the world here being the home and family relationships. It is here in the home, in the early years of parenthood, that the husband and wife may learn some of the deepest realities of human relationship, and the child may actually become their teacher if they are able and willing to learn. For the child is constantly saying something of importance to adults if they can see and hear and feel with him. This is an emotional kind of learning, and it may call for changed attitudes on the part of the parent. Through the nurture of the child the parent himself may grow to be a more genuine person.

The child makes a continual contribution to the growth of the parent even as the parent nurtures the child. Erikson's principle of mutual self-regulation is sound; a similar principle is in Christian insight. In a sound approach to the pastoral care of the parents of young children, either in groups or individually, the pastor and parents alike would discover the forces which actually operate in parent-child relationships and the relation of these to the Christian faith. There is no area in which sound Christian insights are likely to have more meaning than here, and if they are not discovered to be meaningful here, there will be deep resistance to the discovery of their meaning in the larger community. If parents are helped in the spiritual nurture of each other and of their children, they will find it possible to respond in positive ways to the needs of others outside their home—in the immediate neighborhood and in distant places. By giving more effective attention to the beginnings of the growth of persons, the Church would have to give less attention later to problems such as alcoholism, divorce, delinquency, mental illness, and the like. But apparently we would rather try, and often fail, to pick up the pieces of broken humanity than to seek to prevent the brokenness in the first place. The major thrust of pastoral care should be at the point of growth. Experience has shown that if we stumble here we are also likely to stumble when we accept cure as our goal.

For those who would ask about methods of pastoral care of the family we suggest small group discussions where parents are permitted to express their feelings and concerns under the kind of leadership which helps them to work out their problems and achieve trust, autonomy, and other ego strengths within themselves. Along with this, some parents would ask for—and need—personal attention in pastoral counseling. The pastor needs adequate training for both of these tasks. Also, he should be able to use other resources in the community.

Erikson as a scientist avoids theological and pastoral implications in his work, and rightly so. He offers us his insights into the nature of human growth, and it is up to the theologian and pastor to bring to his work their own problems and insights, and to ask about relationships. This should be done, not just on the level of ideas, but with ideas which grow out of the close observation of life processes. Never in reading Erikson are we allowed to forget that he is a clinician, and that he is trying to state what he finds in his clinical practice. He is not just spinning theories. In method too, he has something to teach the pastor.

The reader certainly has not failed to ask the significance of Erikson's characterization of the first ego crisis as "basic trust or mistrust" for the Christian experience of faith. Basic trust is the beginning of ego growth, and a necessary element in each succeeding stage. The Christian faith insists that salvation is through faith, and faith is a person's self-committing response to the grace of God. What is the relation of the experience of basic trust in Erikson's meaning to faith in the Christian sense? To ask this question may seem to be heresy in some quarters, but it needs to be asked. One might make the further observation that the Christian faith often seems to be fixated on the idea of salvation through faith. Many Christian interpreters never seem to get beyond this particular formula. Is there nothing more to Christian experience? What is the relation, for example, of Christian faith to the ego crises of autonomy or initiative, or to the remaining crises—or to the negative aspects of these stages? Are Christian interpreters stressing faith as the beginning aspect of Christian experience, to the exclusion of other aspects which are important for the maturing ego? What would be the meaning of the much used phrase, "growth in grace," in the light of ego development? Could it be that one reason for the lack of power so frequently discovered in the lives of Christians is the failure to relate their faith in a living way to their own processes of growth? Without in any way discounting or minimizing the importance of faith, theological correlations need to be made with the qualities of the maturing ego, and pastors should be trained to understand the relation between Christian growth and ego growth. One would hardly expect to find a creative, mature Christian experience in a person of childish or immature ego development.

Similar questions could be asked theologically and pastorally at each stage of development. At times preachers exhort their congregations to an interpretation of the Christian faith requiring submission to the will of God in a manner which would demand the surrender of autonomy. Some Christian hymns embody this idea. But it is becoming clear that the development of autonomy in early childhood is one of the marks of a strong person. To what extent do we unwittingly teach the identification of the will of God with pseudo-autonomous drives which would be unacceptable if seen as part of the self? On the other hand, is not a genuine exercise of autonomy essential to any deep and creative Christian commitment? Who can give that of which he has not yet come into possession? May not this be the reason for many "decisions" which fall by the wayside?

For many persons, crises of doubt continue throughout life. Many great Christian leaders, such as Luther, were assailed by strong doubts. When we reject a person's doubts we reject a living, though negative, aspect of a person's ego. In accepting and understanding a person who has doubts, we help him to face, and either live with or resolve, the conflicts which lead to doubt. Doubts about God cannot be separated from doubts about oneself, and doubt is part of the experience of every person.

Genuine commitment, the commitment made in self-giving love and trust, is not an act performed at a given moment, but a basic quality of relationships which develops slowly, in little events of life, beginning in early childhood.

Commitment is a response of trust, autonomy, and initiative to day-by-day relationships which are trustworthy, permit freedom, and encourage concern for others. There is a time in late adolescence when genuine commitment may become a matter of conscious decision, but such a decision grows from within. It is in adult life that the meaning of commitment becomes explicit in many daily relationships. Here its genuine nature is attested by spontaneity and warmth in ordinary relationships or conditions, and by deep courage and strength under stress. Pastoral care given by genuinely committed persons—parents, pastors, laymen —is the climate in which deeply committed persons may grow. But such persons will be committed to persons, values, and relationships, rather than to institutions or creeds. And therefore they will have a basis in their own being for understanding the meaning of commitment to Christ.

Many questions could be raised regarding the theological and pastoral implications of Erikson's third ego crisis, initiative or guilt. Consider the guilt experienced by the young child because he wants something which is forbidden. Is this guilt before God? We have known children of this age who were in terror about what they had been told about God. These children apparently related their guilt feelings, which are a normal part of this age, to what they had been told about God. When, if ever, is guilt developed in relationship to parents to be identified as guilt before God? And can the guilt feelings engendered at this early age be more fully released through the symbolic forms of religion or through a less symbolic process?

A further question is: What is the meaning of love in the life of the child? Certainly the infant needs a kind of care that a five-year-old would find objectionable, but at each age a kind of love is needed which gives the child a sense of belonging with those who care for him, and which thus overcomes his sense of separation. He must have meaning to others, and they to him. The stage of initiative is one in which the child is learning to love others in a way he has never experienced before. If he is made to feel excessively guilty about this, or if sufficient trust and autonomy has not accrued in the earlier years, he may not have the strength to handle his guilt feelings constructively. Or if the mother has been emotionally seductive to the male child, an extra burden of anxiety and guilt is placed upon him. The child learns what love means through the kind of love he receives. From the depths of his being he wants to love in the sense of feeling a warmth, closeness, and unity with persons in his surroundings.

The pastor and the Church are committed to teach the way of love. Christian love, as exemplified in Christ, is a self-giving concerned with the needs of others, seeking no reward for itself, and not only to refrain from harming others, but to creatively contribute to their welfare and lead to a sense of community. It seeks unity through a genuine concern and respect for the other person which permits him freedom. Such love cannot be taught by precepts. Children understand it when they experience it from others and learn to be loving in return. But such love must be specific; that is, it must be concerned with real needs; and real needs may differ. Thus the love given an infant may be different from that given a six-year-old. It is these differences which need to be spelled out in the lives of parents and children, and this is part of the task of pastoral care. Parents can accomplish much of this themselves, if given freedom in small-group discussions.

But we in the Church have often worked against ourselves. We have taught the need for love, but we have made people feel guilty about loving. We have done this through our attitudes toward sex, transmitted from parents to children. Children who are taught that their bodies are dirty and evil in the toilet training experience come to the stage of initiative with guilt already formed. When feelings relating to sex and love emerge, and especially if these feelings are rejected by the parent, more guilt is generated. Or if the new feelings receive too much acceptance and satisfaction from the parent, they may become threatening to the child. To cope with his guilt and anxiety the child may withdraw his feelings from the parent. He loses initiative. He no longer can reach out for the satisfaction of his needs. And as he grows up he becomes an adult who cannot love. This can create serious problems in the search for ego identity in adolescence or the search for intimacy in the young-adult period. He hears a sermon on love and devoutly wishes that he could love, but feels inwardly blocked. Many of the problems of human relationship grow out of this situation. The Church and the pastor need to examine their theology of sex and love, and particularly pastoral attitudes, to eliminate those elements which tend to create excessive and unrealistic guilt feelings in relation to love and sex, and to discover what needs to be done in our culture to help persons experience that form of love which is appropriate to their particular stage of life.

We used the phrase "excessive and unrealistic" in relation to guilt feelings in order to distinguish the constructive uses of guilt. For guilt and guilt feelings are not altogether evil. Like other aspects of life, they have a real purpose, which may become unhealthy when they are excessive or related to feelings rather than actions. But a person may be unhealthy also because he does not experience adequate and appropriate guilt feelings. He may have committed an act which is obviously harmful or destructive, but show no remorse. Indeed, a person may put on a front of good behavior in order to cover up his real values. Guilt in its healthy use becomes somewhat analogous to fever in the organism, an inner signal that something is wrong and needs to be corrected. As such, it is a part of every healthy person, since no one is perfect. But when guilt develops excessively, when it is used as a reason for self-punishment rather than self-change, or when guilt-producing structures are absent or do not function, then illness is in process. The Christian faith does not condone guilt. The forgiveness symbolized in the Cross requires change as part of the process of repentance and accepted forgiveness. Thus the Christian answer to guilt involves understanding, acceptance, and growth to a higher synthesis. Guilt is a signal for the need for growth.

By the time a child has reached six, he has thoroughly experienced two profound aspects of life, good and evil. It could be hoped that the good might outbalance the evil in the life of every child, but this obviously is not so. From early infancy both good and evil have been mediated through the parents and other representatives of society—since no human being can be perfect. The Church has been much concerned with the problem of good and evil, but all too often the concern has been expressed theologically rather than practically or pastorally. The child, and the adult as well, has a need to project evil into the world in personifications, such as the evil parent, teacher, foreigner, or representative of another race or class. In religion, evil has been personified as Satan or as a demonic spirit.

One of the tasks of pastoral care is to help individuals distinguish between real evil and supposed evil. Real evil, the truly demonic, is those attitudes, relationships, and actions which destroy oneself or others. Sometimes these may be clothed in the most righteous rationalizations. Supposed evil has numerous psychological roots, but there is a large element of narcissism in it. That which I do not want or which denies some of my desires seems to be evil. And it is usually necessary, for the sake of internal comfort, to project this evil on other persons or objects, often including God.

Another aspect of the pastoral task of helping persons distinguish between real and supposed evil is to enable persons to experience in relationship what the Bible describes as the love which overcomes evil. The Biblical solution of the problem of evil is never repression or denial, but frank and open admission and honesty. This is always in the light of a forgiving, reconciling God, in whose love, experienced through human relationships, there is strength to overcome evil. Sometimes in childhood and in childish adults the law must be used to restrain the expression of evil. But the essence of the New Testament solution is that a person should grow up to the maturity which is in Christ, so that the control of evil is a spontaneous experience emerging from within, directed by the desire for reconciliation. And as Erikson's characterization of the stages of growth remind us, there is an evil aspect to each stage, and so the conflict between destructive and constructive forces may continue throughout life. This problem is never settled once and for all. It is constant and continuous, changing only in form. Its solution is in a deep personal identity that yields a constructive motivation through which evil is taken up into the good, and a new synthesis is created within the individual. The Biblical injunction to overcome evil with good needs to be translated into the actualities of every stage of growth.

There are many other points at which questions of theological and pastoral correlation could be raised. One more comment will be ventured. Erikson goes to biology for the basis of his epigenetic principle of development, a principle which holds that there are present in the organism basic structures which at an optimal time will emerge if life conditions permit. Thus a person is not just the result of his experiences, but also of what he brings to those experiences in terms of emerging capacities. This is a corrective for that kind of psychology which sees a person as nothing more than a stimulus-and-response mechanism. But more important, there are theological correlations. For Christian theology has always held to something given in the nature of man. On the positive side this has been expressed in such symbols as "the image of God," and on the negative side as man's propensity to sin.

Sin has been interpreted as the failure to fulfill the potentials of the self in relationship to God. The presence of a structure within the human personality makes the fulfillment of the potentiality of that structure obligatory. The individual's inner being demands fruition, or else there is sin, destructiveness, and death. Reflection on Erikson's last stage of ego growth, that of final integrity or despair, in the light of a clinical knowledge of older persons, should help one understand the meaning of a basic structure in life, whether formulated biologically, psychologically, or theologically.

Christian theology has taken exception to a theory of the ego which holds that its primary purpose is adaptation to the world. Erikson's concept of ego development takes us beyond mere adaptation. The development of individual potentials is at stake. Furthermore, the individual ego has some power to change the world rather than adapt to it. One of the strong impulses of youth is to change the world, and this should be understood not only as a projection of the youth's need to change himself or as a sign of his hostility, but also as an unarticulated insight that something in the world really needs to be changed. For there is something wrong in a society or group which fails to give youth the foundation for a viable sense of personal identity. There is such a thing as creative adaptation, which adapts to the environment by changing it. Pastors should recognize that persons will be likely to have a distorted view of, and relationship to, any ultimate or transcendant loyalties as long as there are serious problems of adaptation in the area of the proximate.

One of the tendencies in the Church and the pastor is to become overly involved in symbolic content and functions, and divorced from the real experiences of persons. Then we go on speaking in theological symbols which our people no longer seem to understand. We have had more than one voice raised lately over the meaninglessness of Christian theological symbols. But the answer is not necessarily in a new set of symbols. Symbols with actual meaning cannot be created by any artificial means, but grow out of dynamic experiences of individuals and groups, and then become reminders to future generations of those events.

Each generation must experience for itself not only the symbol but the reality and meaning in the symbol. In the task of mediating the Gospel to persons, the pastor needs to be deeply concerned with the realities of the Gospel and of human experience equally. Symbolic structure has creative meaning only when there is something in experience to be structured. Symbolism becomes an element in the formation of neurotic processes when symbol is divorced from inner experience and meaning and allowed to proliferate in a vacuum. This has happened in the past generation, and creative pastoral care is needed to bring vitality of meaning back into Christian experience.

�֍ 6 �֍
The Making of a Pastor

THIS chapter is not to be a discussion of the whole of theological education, but only of certain aspects which seem pertinent to the theme we have been developing.

A vital and creative Christian experience in the making of a pastor is clearly essential. The fact that many students enter seminary without such experience should not be held against them, but should be seen as a challenge to the school. Many of these men have come seeking this experience, and of course they find it is not available through the academic process. This obviously is not the purpose of the academic study of religion, but often the young student has serious misconceptions on this point.

By a vital and creative Christian experience, we mean one which gives meaning to the total life and work of the pastor, and to his human relationships. Since it is grounded in a personal faith and commitment to God as He is in Christ, it is an experience which gives the person a solid sense of identity before God, and therefore before man. It is an experience which leads him to openness toward himself and his own motivations rather than to a projection of his anxiety, guilt, or hostility onto others. At his age he cannot be expected to have achieved a fully mature love, but he has a sense of his need for growth in this respect. His experience of forgiveness is still progressing. He has not yet arrived. He is searching for a new understanding of himself and his relationships with others, and he is conscious of his need to overcome whatever obstacles he may face in deepening his relationships to others. He has the kind of honest appreciation of both his own strengths and his weaknesses which is the basis of humility. He has some awareness of his tendency to manipulate others in order to avoid facing his own problems. His life is open to the influence of the Holy Spirit, so that the fruits of the Spirit are gradually becoming realized in him. He has a sense of the genuine freedom of the Christian person, but subjects himself to the fundamental discipline of a love which demands that he seek for others what he seeks for himself. He does not feel under compulsion to accept, and to insist that others accept, a specific formulation of Christian experience, but he is concerned with the reality behind any theological formulation. This statement is far from exhaustive, but it will serve to emphasize that the roots of pastoral care are in Christian experience.

Our emphasis on communication through relationships is not to be taken to mean that vigorous intellectual training and mastery of intellectual disciplines are not important for the pastor. Emphasis on intellectual training can be detrimental to the pastor when it excludes relational aspects of the ministry as unimportant. On the other hand, many mistakes are made by "well-intentioned" pastors who lack knowledge. Genuine love toward God and man includes both knowing them directly and knowing about them. Thus the pastor needs to be a highly intelligent person who has subjected himself to the discipline of study. Absence of this background will tend to destroy the trust of others in him. Sound knowledge is one dimension of a helping relationship with his people.

One of the needs of seminaries today is to learn what it means to promote the growth of the whole man rather than merely to give lip service to this idea. Such ideas as "the growth of the whole man" easily catch the imagination, but enthusiasm wanes when specific suggestions are made for implementing them. On the whole, theological education tends to be very conservative, and to follow the Church rather than furnish leadership. Or it may tend to confine its leadership to the realm of ideas, and discount the world of functional realities.

One of the fundamental questions raised by the pastoral-care movement is: What should be the perspective of theological education in its curriculum-building and its teaching? The standard answer given by most seminaries to this question is scholarship. The seminary is a community of scholars; each member of the faculty is expected to be a scholar in his particular field. Latest findings in Biblical, theological, historical, and other aspects of scholarship in religion are brought to the student. European scholarship is highly revered in the seminary, and sometimes idolized. In fact, scholarship often is rated much more highly than the ability to be a good teacher.

But there is a certain dilemma in the scholarship perspective. How is it to be made meaningful and relevant to the pastor and the problems of persons? This dilemma is often reflected in the inability of the student to see the relevance of what he is studying for what he hopes to do, or is doing, in the pastorate. Part of this failure may be owing to the student's lack of experience, but in part it is because scholarship is relevant to scholarship, but not necessarily to the problems of the pastorate. Some of the problems of Biblical and theological scholarship are so far removed from the problems of human existence that no amount of imagination can make them relevant. Quite justifiably scholarly problems have to do with technical issues in a given field, not with what goes on in persons and between persons or between persons and God.

One of the serious effects of the scholarship perspective upon the personality of the theological student is a confused sense of identity. Many students come to seminary with some confusion as to their personal and professional identity. Three or four years of study under "scholars" forces them in a position of either identifying with these teachers and accepting themselves as scholars or rejecting this identity for themselves. For those of high intellectual capacity, such positive identification is not as difficult as it is for those with more limited capacities, and academic rewards are a further encouragement. This student then sees himself as essentially a "scholar and teacher" (these activities are closely associated in our culture), rather than as a pastor. The student who takes a negative stand toward scholarship (and some men of high ability do this because of conflicting personality needs) tends to discount learning for the pastor and work on his hunches, or to give his own personal needs full control of his work. This negative identity—what the individual feels he should not be—is frequently expressed in the seminary graduate who stops studying seriously after leaving seminary. The question we are raising here is this: What basis for identity as a pastor—in the full meaning of this term—does the scholarship perspective offer the theological student? Does it lead him away from responsible functioning as a pastor?

Let it not be assumed that in raising this question we are against scholarship in the seminary. We are decidedly for it, and at certain points would add to it; but this is not the issue. The issue is: How, in an atmosphere of scholarship, can the student gain a positive basis for identity as a pastor? How, in an atmosphere which emphasizes books, ideas, examinations, grades, intellectual controversies and issues, and the necessary technical aspects of scholarship—how, in the atmosphere of the academy—do we help the student get a working and workable image of himself as a pastor? To say that much of the scholarship in the seminary deals with the existential problems of life, with which the pastor also deals, misses the point. For the academic approach of the seminary deals with these issues—sin, salvation, guilt, hate, love, death, suffering, and the like—intellectually, academically, and rationally, and often comes out with formulations which are of no value to a person in the actual throes of suffering. The perspective from which we deal with the issues is the point here. For example, a philosophical or theological course on the problem of suffering may help a student to think through some of the intellectual problems related to suffering, to evaluate various interpretations and notions about suffering, and to clear away a lot of hazy thinking on the subject. But when he faces a person who is suffering, he will need to be not a philosopher, but a pastor such as we have been describing in this book. Intellectual discipline should be one aspect of the pastor's training, but by itself it is insufficient for his needs.

How then can the scholarly emphasis of the seminary be utilized to help the student develop an identity as a pastor, the kind of identity he needs if he is to become a real pastor and not something else? The answer which we shall give to this problem will hardly be acceptable to most seminary faculties. For the fact is that the very qualities which make a man a good scholar may not be those which make a good pastor, and every man has to use the talents he has been given.

However, our suggestion is this, that seminary teachers should not only be scholars, they should also be pastors. By this is meant that they should have a continuing responsibility as pastors with one congregation—part time, of course—and thus become involved deeply in the life of one congregation. Of course they would have to have assistance, depending on the size of the parish, but in some cases their students could be given a creative learning experience by serving as their assistants. Such relationships would give the student a basis for developing an identity as a pastor. He would see his teacher not only as a scholar but as a pastor, a pastor whose scholarship finds expression in his pastoral pursuits. The frequent complaint about the irrelevance of so much scholarship would no longer be heard. Such relationships would bring new perspectives on curriculum-planning and teaching and give the teacher the material through which he could integrate, in reality rather than in the abstract, the area of his scholarship with the actual situation in the parish.

We shall not deal here with the objections which will be launched against this idea. Some of these will be real and some fanciful, but they are obstacles to be overcome if theological education is to bring new life into the Church. The teacher in the seminary may see himself as a pastor, but the student does not see him this way. The seminary today has identified itself with the academy—and the teacher with the academician—rather than with the profession for which it is seeking to train men. This is the situation which needs to be modified. We are not offering a blueprint of how this is to be done, since it will be achieved, if at all, in terms of differing local conditions and denominational polity. It is obvious that our suggestion would bring radical changes in the structure of theological education which could be worked out only with considerable time and experiment.

Not only does the faculty need continual encounter with the life of a parish, but so does the student! Theological education today is grounded on a very serious fallacy, namely that ideas and values become incorporated in the functioning processes of the student through verbal communication. On the contrary, both general observation and scientific studies indicate clearly that for creative learning the student must become involved in the processes and structures he is studying.[1] Very frequently the theological student has not had experience in the area in which a professor is lecturing. Therefore the professor's ideas sound unreal, or completely irrelevant, or even threatening. The student may learn them by rote and pass his examinations, but be unable to incorporate them into his thinking and acting. Or he may find himself unable to learn these ideas—without understanding why. The student who fights with unreal or threatening ideas may come out better in the long run if he permits himself to be motivated by his irritation to continue the struggle with his problem. Ideas, attitudes, and values are learned or changed only in situations where teacher and student are both involved in a third dimension, that is, the reality which is under consideration.

This means that the curriculum and teaching of the seminary must be grounded in the involvement of the teacher and student in the ongoing life of a parish. The layman must of necessity become a part of this process, since he is the center of the life of the parish. It is for him that sermons are given, educational programs projected, services of worship held, funerals and weddings conducted. It is his growth and welfare with which we are concerned, his salvation for which we pray, and his understanding of the faith that merits the pastor's attention. The deep crises met in pastoral care are those in the lives of laymen, whether death or illness or some other kind of emotional and spiritual separation. The layman is being told that he should carry the message of the Gospel into the community, into business and into the world. But he must be equipped in mind and spirit to do this.

It is amazing that theological education can proceed with so little concern for the persons with whom the pastor is to work: the laymen in his church and the persons in his community. Thus it is not surprising to hear ministers complain about the demands and needs of the laymen as though these were burdens. To inadequately trained and improperly oriented ministers these demands are burdens, not opportunities. It is not surprising that laymen think that theological education is missing the point!

Teacher, student, and layman need to become involved in a living encounter in the task of theological education. Curriculum and teaching should be organized around the experience of the student and teacher in actual parish situations, with actual persons. This calls for a radical departure from the present methods of the seminary. The new approach would go far beyond what is usually called "field work," since it would include all departments. There is a gnawing conviction in the minds of many theological professors today that we are failing to reach our students in any profound way. To overcome this anxiety we add more courses, increase requirements, and do other such things to bolster up a curriculum and methodology which needs radical change. Theological education needs to be centered on the involvement of student, layman, and teacher with each other and with the Christian faith.

Let it be clear that we are not suggesting more "experience" for theological students in a church. Many students today are getting experience in student charges, but they do not have the foggiest idea as to how to relate their "experience" to their studies in the seminary. Furthermore, their experience is only a vague reality. They do not know how to go about discovering its meaning because they are unable to see what is there. In counseling courses it is usual to have students report on their interviews, which they have recorded verbatim; but they often do not see the meaning of what they have written down. The same lack of meaning is true in other aspects of their parish experience.

This does not intend to be critical of the students. For they are the products of an educational system which has taught them ideational structure, but has not enabled them to understand reality and its functioning. They have been taught to be dependent on their teachers and not to take initiative in thinking, and they have learned this lesson well. They have also been taught that imagination is a wonderful tool, but that it should be used very sparingly since we must deal with facts. Therefore they cannot see relationships between facts, and they cannot understand meanings and values beyond facts. Also, they have been carefully taught to repress their own feelings and emotional conflicts and to exercise various psychological defenses, with the result that they cannot enter empathically into the experiences of other persons and participate in their meanings and sufferings. Theological education tends to reinforce these inadequate teachings.

Students need help to discover what they are experiencing: to face and understand the feelings and reactions this event arouses in them and then to seek to understand what it means to others who are involved; to ask what it means in the light of the Christian faith and what is needed to enable others to enter into creative Christian meanings. The student needs help in penetrating beneath the verbalisms of the faith to the very real and creative processes and meanings to which these verbalisms may point. Since such help is essentially the task of the teacher, the teacher himself is required to be involved experientially in all of the crucial issues of a parish, and to some extent in the life of the student. The task of the teacher is not to pour ideas into the mind of the student, but to awaken in him the latent processes that lead to insight and understanding.

Again we are offering no blueprint for such theological education. Here and there it is already being carried out in the work of individual teachers. The full impact of what we are saying may have to wait for a new generation of teachers who have participated in such learning experiences as students. We are not suggesting that the ancient and revered "content" of theological education be ruled out. But by some means there needs to be a creative synthesis of content with real pastoral involvement, in which these dimensions of religious faith are permitted to speak to each other. Such speaking will take place through the mind and heart of the student and teacher in a mutual learning encounter—one in which the student is given the freedom and responsibility to combine a Christian interpretation of life with daring imagination, and is helped to cultivate a spirit sensitive to human need. This means the deep involvement of the student teacher, and layman around the profound issues of human life and the life of the Church, past, present, and in the immediate future. To be sure, the ultimate dimensions of the Christian faith must become both the motivation and the goal of such an educational process, but again these must find expression and be authenticated in living persons rather than in verbal structure. For the Word of God is a Person—a Living Person—or, as Paul says, our faith is futile (I Cor. 15:17-19).

We have already indicated the need for extending the scholarly pursuits of the seminary. We believe this should be done in the area of what is known today as the behavioral sciences—

psychology, psychiatry, and the dynamics of personality-culture relationships. Again we do not offer a blueprint for carrying this out, since there is more than one way. However, the main concern is that it be done.

This emphasis is not entirely missing in seminary curriculums today. However, considering the function the pastor might fulfill in the lives of persons, much more stress needs to be given in this area. Furthermore, the pastor should be familiar with, and be able to utilize, some of the methods and approaches of these disciplines. For the pastor is in an exceedingly strategic position in the field of human growth. He stands in a crucial position between individual and cultural dynamics and no profession has more opportunity for either good or evil influence than his. But more than this, the pastor can render much of his religious ministry ineffective by not having a basic and workable knowledge of the individual, social, and cultural influences which shape human life in his church and community. Furthermore, the pastor needs to have an appreciation of the work of the leaders in the behavioral science fields.

This last point is important. One of the intellectual dangers of theological education is that an attempt is made to put knowledge through a critical analysis from a given theological point of view. There is necessity and value in this. But such an analysis must proceed not only from an understanding of theology, but also from within the field which is being evaluated. Otherwise, many of the negative criticisms offered will be as absurd as some of the theological criticisms of psychoanalysis have been in the past. They have been made out of anxiety or hostility rather than of understanding. But even more important, the behavioral sciences are here to stay, and they will see great development in the years ahead. The love of truth which the Christian faith commands should teach us to appreciate the positive contribution of these sciences to the work of the Church and lead us to use their contribution for the benefit of persons.

There is another aspect of this problem. Those theologies which consider themselves immune to criticism and evaluation from other points of view will eventually lead nowhere. For theological concepts, like concepts in any field, need to expand and grow in meaning, or else they become dead. The behavioral sciences are producing material which should be considered, and to some extent related to the theological concept of man. Part of the task of the seminary is to help the student begin this process of synthesis. We say "begin," because this is a lifelong process, not to be confined to the years of seminary experience.

The danger that some will see here is that we turn the student away from his central task as a pastor and make him into a psychologist or an "amateur psychiatrist." This is a part of the problem of idenity discussed above. Some students come to seminary with a strong sense of pastoral identity—they want to go into the pastorate to help persons. At some point in their earlier Christian experience they have caught this vision. Their training in seminary, however, does not seem to fit them for this task, and when they get into the parish they find many obstacles, one of the chief being their lack of training in fields which help them to understand persons. So somewhere along the line, in seminary or in the early years of their ministry, they shift their vocational plans and enter one of the other helping professions. Or they leave the parish ministry and go into some form of specialized ministry such as hospital chaplaincy or pastoral counseling. The real problem here is not that they have been taught something which is foreign to the ministry. It is that they have not been trained adequately to help persons as pastors, and then they may have found the organizational structure of their church operating against such activities. One answer to this problem is better education in the behavioral sciences, a more effective integration of this education with the theological perspective, and more effective training in the arts and skills of helping persons as pastors. It has been my privilege to enter deeply into the experiences of a number of such students and pastors, and I have never found a man leaving the ministry because his training in the behavioral sciences was too great or his skills in helping others too effective. There is a tragic attrition in the parish ministry, but for other reasons.

Another essential approach in the making of pastors is clinical pastoral training. We will not repeat at length the various testimonials to the value of clinical pastoral training. It is sufficient to point out that such training, when carried out properly, cannot be reproduced in the classroom. Nor is there any other kind of theological training which produces the same values. The major advantage of clinical pastoral training is experience in personal and pastoral relationships under supervision. In the classroom we can *talk* about relationships; but in clinical pastoral training the student *experiences* relationships in a context in which he is helped to understand what is actually going on between himself and others. The fact that in this case the others are either persons who are sick in one way or another, or they are fellow students or professional helpers such as doctors and nurses, gives the student and the supervisor the opportunity to explore various kinds of relationships which are experienced by the student. Of course, the central problem is the relationship of patient and pastor. Theological education needs to accept and act upon the fact that the discussion of relationships in the classroom is no substitute for the actual experience of relationships under supervision. And no other branch of theological education has developed the art and practice of supervision in relationships more fully than has clinical pastoral education.

Today there is a movement toward what is being called "clinical pastoral training in the parish." It might be better if the word "clinical" were left off; on the other hand, its use does indicate that the methods developed by the clinical pastoral training movement are being applied in the parish. This is all to the good—just what is needed to transform the seminary "field work" of the past into a meaningful educational experience. There are special problems in such training in the parish which are far from being surmounted today, although there are some encouraging experiments.

One basic problem for the seminary in the clinical pastoral training movement, whether in the institution or in the parish, is the development of supervisors and the relation of the supervisors to the seminary faculty. Among the conditions making for an uneven quality of supervision, in the clinical pastoral training movement as a whole, are: the rapid growth of the movement in the past decade, the process of accrediting supervisors, the refusal or inability of the seminaries to become deeply involved in clinical pastoral training, the fear in some quarters of what they describe as an undue psychiatric emphasis in clinical pastoral training. A closer cooperation between the seminary and local centers, with the inclusion of the clinical training supervisor in the regular faculty of the seminary, would make for real advances. As long as clinical pastoral training is kept on the periphery of theological education it will not be able to make its full contribution.

We have aready referred to the professional importance of the pastor's identity as a person. A pastor needs a clear and firm sense of himself as a man and a person as a basis for entering into the experiences of others in a pastoral relationship.

To elaborate on the problems involved in the struggle for ego identity in American youth is beyond the scope of this chapter. Many theological students suffer from the same kinds of identity conflict as do many other young men in our culture. This may be due to weaknesses in the culture which prevent it from offering a solid basis for identity. Or it may be due to conflicts in youth which prevents them from accepting the identity the culture provides. It may be grounded in inadequate interpersonal relationships. At least, many youths in our culture grow up without experiencing a deep sense of their value and meaning to themselves and to others. This frequently finds expression in vocational conflict and inability to make vocational decisions. It also finds expression in sexual conflicts, an extreme example of which would be the youth who prefers homosexual contacts. And it also finds expression in youth's approach to religion. Many of the religious problems of this age—problems of belief, of faith, of action—are rooted in the inability of the young person to discover who he is before others and before God. Erikson's description of the identity conflict in Martin Luther, in *Young Man Luther*,[2] has many parallels in theological students today. Bowers, in *Conflicts in the Clergy*,[3] gives a picture of some extreme examples of identity conflicts in ministers, counterparts of which are to be found in any theological seminary.

The theological student brings his problems of identity, mild or severe, with him to the school.[4] And consciously or unconsciously he seeks to work them out in the academic experience. This means that his study of theology, Bible, and other seminary disciplines is motivated by deep personal needs of which he may or may not be aware. In attempting to resolve intellectual problems, he is trying also to discover who he is and his relation to knowledge. Thus, wrestling intellectually with the problem of God, or of guilt, or of the meaning of life, or of history, or of being, to mention just a few possibilities, he is also wrestling with something very important within himself. He is seeking so-called "objective" knowledge as a basis and guide for subjective experiences. And he may be projecting a great many of his own feelings and conflicts onto "objective" knowledge, so that what he believes to be objective is really more the reflection of his own inner world. Or he may find that academic requirements seriously interfere with his personal pursuit of truth as determined by his own needs. Here again he may face the problem of following his own sense of being or of conforming to cultural demands. If he does the former, he may fail in his studies; if he does the latter, he will sacrifice his own integrity and accept dependence on authorities for what no authority can really give him.

The way in which the student resolves this problem, both emotionally and intellectually, will have far-reaching effects on his capacity to become a pastor. For whatever pastoral relationships he creates with others will in part reflect the kind of solution he has found to this problem.

The seminary therefore needs to see its academic functions in the light of the profound need of the student to find an intellectual frame of reference in which he can stand, and from which he can function in the process of discovering his own identity. This means that the seminary must combine its academic purpose with something of a therapeutic purpose. We are speaking of the emotional and intellectual climate of the classroom, of the teacher-student relationship, of the opportunity of the student to pursue some of his own interests and needs, and of teachers who are more concerned with helping the student learn *how* to think that with *what* he thinks. There is no doubt that many seminary students are searching for these values in their intellectual experience. Nor is there any doubt that some teachers are aware of this and are assisting students creatively. But the situation needs a wider recognition and a more conscious provision for its constructive handling throughout the total process of theological education.

If the seminary is truly interested in the "whole man," it has another responsibility which in no way conflicts with its intellectual task. Theological education must become as concerned for the emotional growth of the student as for his intellectual growth, and make adequate provisions for helping him on this level. A highly trained intellect in an emotionally immature or sick person can be destructive in the ministry. Students with the kind of mild emotional patterns which handicap them in their personal relationships should also be a focus of concern.

There is no one approach to this problem. Essentially the student needs an experience of self-discovery, that is, self-understanding and the kind of growth which comes through this process, or at least an opportunity for this experience. Some opportunities may occur in certain kinds of classes, some in worship, some in various small-group experiences. However, a more systematic approach would be through a staff of well-trained pastoral counselors, supplemented by psychotherapists where needed. A question here is the level of personal help to students for which a school should accept responsibility, and the point at which the student should be asked to accept the financial responsibility. We are not advocating that seminaries make long psychotherapy available to its students without cost.

One of the needs of the theological student in his first year is the opportunity to examine his motives for going into the ministry, and the suitability of his kind of person for the work of the pastor. A staff of pastoral counselors should be available for this. For many theological students a relatively short period of counseling would be sufficient for needed insight and growth. Others would require a longer period.

The value of this approach for the teaching program of the seminary needs to be explored. However, it would seem that theological education should begin not only with what great thinkers have said, but also with what the student believes and says. Until the student has come to terms with himself religiously and theologically, he is hardly in a position to really appreciate the contribution of others. Theological study which is not accompanied by sufficient opportunity for personal insight may become a matter of rationalization and projection—the more brilliant the intellect, the more proficient in this. For deep, unconscious reasons, a student may find himself inordinately drawn toward one particular authority or position, while he is repelled by others which really deserve his unbiased consideration. Also, some students must settle emotional conflicts with their parents before they are really in a position to clarify their faith or relationship with God. This is not an intellectual process and is less likely to take place in a classroom than in a counseling process. Religious and theological studies may become so entangled with unconscious hostilities, anxieties, and guilt feelings that the student is either driven compulsively or blocked and inhibited, without knowing why. Or, as we have indicated previously, a student may succeed in divorcing his intellect from his feelings, and pursue a cold, intellectual, so-called objective approach to religious thought, while his emotional life remains childish or even infantile. Genuine objectivity in matters of vital concern to pastoral care is grounded in a positive faith, a fairly unambivalent commitment, and mature love. It is not devoid of feeling and not coldly objective.

And we should not neglect the value of this approach for the teaching of subjects in the field of pastoral care. So many of the problems in church administration and field-work supervision resolve themselves into problems of personal attitude and relationship. The teaching of preaching, religious education, and counseling is so much more than the teaching of techniques and intellectual content. It is helping the student grow emotionally until he becomes a person who can enter adequately into the teaching or preaching or counseling tasks required of him. Instead of the multiplication of courses and the lengthening of the seminary program, more attention given to the emotional growth of the student would contribute greatly to his effectiveness as a teacher or preacher, or in any aspect of pastoral care. It would also remove obstacles to learning, and hence decrease certain curricular pressures.

Much of what we have been saying in this chapter may be symbolized by the two words, "scholar" and "saint." The symbol which expresses the goals of most theological schools today is the scholar. Strong pressure in this direction is felt from within the schools and from other academic disciplines. But we need to ask just what is this scholarship that the pastor needs? Could it be that we are trying to project into theological education some kinds and areas of scholarship which are not relevant to the pastoral task even though they may have some connection with religion? And could it be that we need to add to the theological curriculum some areas of scholarship which are now being neglected?

But deeper than this, we need to balance the symbol "scholar" with another symbol, "saint." By saint we mean a person who is growing in genuine love toward God and man, who is honestly trying to cope with the conditions in himself which are obstacles to such love, and who is able and willing to use professional services to this end. He is one who takes seriously the statement of Jesus about removing the beam from our own eye so we can see clearly to remove the mote from our brother's eye. He is not only a man who "knows" in the sense of scholarship, but he knows in the sense of the ability to enter directly and deeply into the experiences of others. He may have been a person who was once seriously sick emotionally, but because he has endured the suffering involved in finding wholeness, he can now enter into the suffering of others, whether in groups or in individual relationships. He is a person who is growing toward the fulfillment in his own person of the words of Paul about the fruits of the Spirit (Gal. 5:22), or the thirteenth chapter of I Corinthians. Pastors should not be scholars only. If they are not saints in the meaning we have expressed here, they will not be genuine pastors. In the last analysis we would have to say that becoming a saint is the work of God, but God has given man a responsibility in the process, and we have been talking about some ways to fulfill that responsibility. Many of the major obstacles to creative pastoral relationships have developed in human experience, and they will be cured through human agencies. It is better from the pastoral point of view that these human agencies be also committed to the Christian faith, although we must add, on the basis of our experience, that this is not absolutely essential. The reality of the curative power of genuine love and understanding is essential.

The Church, Christian theology, and theological education today is very concerned about the great problems of our culture, the problems of war and peace, of human justice and welfare, of health and illness, of marriage and the family, and of economic conflict, to mention only a few. Every pastor grows up in a culture, and being human he is likely to participate in the illnesses of that culture. The Church must necessarily make pronouncements on various social problems so that the world knows where it stands. But it faces a greater challenge. Can it devise a means of theological education of the whole man to help its future pastors become comparatively free of the illnesses of their culture, so that in turn they may become effective Christian pastors to persons in that culture and thus help to cure some if its illnesses? For without discounting the value of social action, in the final analysis the cure of the illnesses of our culture will depend upon helping individual persons to become whole, in the New Testament meaning of that phrase.

Notes

Chapter 1. *The Biblical Basis of Pastoral Care*

1. See James D. Smart, *The Rebirth of the Ministry* (Philadelphia: Westminster Press, 1960).
2. Seward Hiltner, *Preface to Pastoral Theology* (New York: Abingdon Press, 1958).
3. Richard Niebuhr, *The Purpose of the Church and Its Ministry* (New York: Harper & Row, 1956).
4. Samuel W. Blizzard, "The Parish Minister's Self-Image of His Master Role," in *Pastoral Psychology*, December, 1958, and also "The Parish Minister's Self-Image and Variability in Community Culture," in *Pastoral Psychology*, October, 1959.

Chapter 2. *The Meaning of Pastoral Care*

1. Alan Richardson, *A Theological Word Book of the Bible* (New York: The Macmillan Company, 1951), p. 100.
2. Paul Althaus, *The So-Called Kerygma and the Historical Jesus*, trans. by David Cairns (London: Oliver and Boyd, 1959), pp. 45-46.
3. James D. Smart, *The Rebirth of the Ministry* (Philadelphia: Westminster Press, 1960), p. 114.
4. George Hendry, *The Holy Spirit in Christian Theology* (Philadelphia: Westminster Press, 1956), p. 98.
5. Quoted by Hendry, *ibid.*, p. 99.
6. John Wesley, Sermon LXXXV, *Works* (London: John Mason, 1830), Vol. VI, p. 512.
7. Paul Tillich, *Systematic Theology*, Vol. II (Chicago: University of Chicago Press, 1957).
8. Edward Thornton, "Health and Salvation," in *The Journal of Religion and Health,* Vol. 2, No. 3.
9. See Dorothy Baruch, *One Little Boy* (New York: Julian Press, 1952), and Gertrud Schwing, *A Way to the Soul of the Mentally Ill,*

trans. by Rudolph Ekstein and Bernard H. Hall (New York: International Universities Press, 1954).

10. Martin Luther, "Treatise on Christian Liberty," *Collected Works* (Philadelphia: A. J. Holman Co., 1951), Vol. 2, p. 338.

11. William Hordern, *A Layman's Guide to Protestant Theology* (New York: The Macmillan Company, 1957).

12. See Hendry, *op. cit.*; F. W. Dillistone, *The Holy Spirit in the Life of Today* (Philadelphia: Westminster Press, 1947); H. Wheeler Robinson, *The Christian Experience of the Holy Spirit* (New York: Harper & Row, 1928); Arnold B. Come, *Human Spirit and Holy Spirit* (Philadelphia: Westminster Press, 1959).

13. Come, *ibid.*, p. 37.

14. Dillistone, *op. cit.*

15. Gertrud Schwing, *op. cit.*, p. 93.

16. Eugene A. Nida, *Message and Mission* (New York: Harper & Row, 1960), p. 226.

Chapter 3. *The Gospel for Persons*

1. The following is just part of a growing literature on the meaning of the personal relationship:
Martin Buber, *I and Thou* (Edinburgh: T. & T. Clark, 1937); John Macmurray, *Persons in Relation* (New York: Harper & Row, 1961); Paul Tournier, *The Meaning of Persons* (New York: Harper & Row, 1957); Rollo May, with Ernest Angel and Henri F. Ellenberger, *Existence* (New York: Basic Books, Inc., 1958); William U. Snyder, *The Psychotherapy Relationship* (New York: The Macmillan Company, 1961).

2. See Arnold B. Come, *Human Spirit and Holy Spirit* (Philadelphia: Westminster Press, 1959).

3. See Eduard Thurneysen, *A Theology of Pastoral Care* (Richmond, Va.: John Knox Press, 1962); Frederic Greeves, *Theology and the Cure of Souls* (Manhasset, N.Y.: Channel Press, 1962).

4. Personal communication.

5. Carl Rogers, *On Becoming a Person* (Boston: Houghton Mifflin Co., 1961).

6. Rollo May, with Ernest Angel and Henri F. Ellenberger, *Existence* (New York: Basic Books, Inc., 1958).

7. A. H. Maslow, *Motivation and Personality* (New York: Harper & Row, 1954).

8. Paul Tillich, *The Courage to Be* (New Haven: Yale University Press, 1952), Chaps. 4 and 5.

9. *Ibid.*, Chap. 6.

10. H. A. Witkin, H. B. Lewis, M. Hertzman, K. Machover, P. Bretnall Meissner, and S. Wapner, *Personality through Perception* (New York: Harper & Row, 1954), p. 469.

11. Clyde Kluckhohn and Henry A. Murray, *Personality in Nature, Society and Culture* (New York: Alfred A. Knopf, 1953). Gordon Allport, *Pattern and Growth in Personality* (New York: Holt, Rinehart and Winston, 1961).

12. Rollo May, *op. cit.*

13. Albert Outler, *Psychotherapy and the Christian Message* (New York: Harper & Row, 1954), Chap. 2.

14. Sigmund Freud, *Collected Papers*, Vol. IV (London: The Hogarth Press and the Institute for Psychoanalysis, 1956).

15. Albert Outler, *op. cit.*, Chap. 4.

16. Calvin S. Hall and Gardner Lindzey, *Theories of Personality* (New York: John Wiley and Sons, Inc., 1957).

17. Harry Stack Sullivan, *The Interpersonal Theory of Psychiatry* (New York: W. W. Norton and Co., 1953).

18. Karen Horney, *Neurosis and Human Growth* (New York: W. W. Norton and Co., 1950), p. 17.

19. Heinz Hartmann, *Essays on Ego Psychology* (New York: International Universities Press, 1964).

20. See "The Ego and Mystic Selflessness" by Herbert Fingarette, in *Identity and Anxiety*, ed. by Maurice R. Stein, Arthur J. Vidich, and David Manning White (Glencoe, Ill.: The Free Press, 1960).

21. D. M. Baillie, *God Was in Christ* (New York: Charles Scribner's Sons, 1955).

22. *Ibid.*, p. 110.

23. *Ibid.*, p. 114.

Chapter 4. *Further Considerations*

1. Eduard Thurneysen, *A Theology of Pastoral Care* (Richmond: The John Knox Press, 1962), p. 15.

2. *Ibid.*, p. 109.

3. *Ibid.*, p. 107.

4. Martin Buber, *Between Man and Man* (New York: The Macmillan Company, 1947); Reuel L. Howe, *The Miracle of Dialogue* (New York: The Seabury Press, 1963).

5. Henry J. Cadbury, *Jesus, What Manner of Man?* (New York: The Macmillan Company, 1947), pp. 94-95.

6. Carl Michalson, *Faith for Personal Crises* (New York: Charles Scribner's Sons, 1958), pp. 12-13.

7. John Calvin, *Institutes of the Christian Religion* (Philadelphia: Presbyterian Board of Education, 1813), 6th Ed., Bk. III, Chap. 2, p. 526.

8. Erik Erikson, *Young Man Luther* (New York: W. W. Norton & Co., 1958), Chap. 5.

9. Some readers will recognize that we are speaking here of a kind of experience described by psychoanalysts as "transference." For further

study of transference see: Carl Menninger, *Theory of Psychoanalytic Technique* (New York: Basic Books, 1958), Chap. 4.

10. For further discussion of words as cues see John Dollard and Neal E. Miller, *Personality and Psychotherapy* (New York: McGraw-Hill Book Company, 1950), pp. 106-9.

11. Philip Watson, *The Concept of Grace* (London: The Epworth Press, 1959), p. 27.

12. Emil Brunner, *The Divine Imperative*, tr. Olive Wyon (Philadelphia: The Westminster Press, 1947), p. 328.

13. Paul Tillich, *Systematic Theology* (Chicago: University of Chicago Press, 1951), Vol. I, p. 286.

Chapter 5. *Pastoral Care and the Growth of Persons*

1. For the traditional approach to pastoral care see: Paul E. Johnson, *Psychology of Pastoral Care* (Nashville: Abingdon Press, 1953); C. W. Brister, *Pastoral Care in the Church* (New York: Harper & Row, 1964); William A. Clebsch and Charles R. Jaekle, *Pastoral Care in Historical Perspective* (Englewood Cliffs, N.J.: Prentice-Hall, Inc., 1964).

2. This is amply illustrated by such books as: Leontine Young, *Out of Wedlock* (New York: McGraw Hill Book Co., 1954); Edrita Fried, *On Love and Sexuality* (New York: Grove Press, 1961); Dorothy W. Baruch, *One Little Boy* (New York: Julian Press, 1952).

3. Clebsch and Jaekle, *op. cit.* (Englewood Cliffs, N.J.: Prentice-Hall, Inc., 1964).

4. O. Hobart Mowrer, *The Crisis in Psychiatry and Religion* (Princeton: D. Van Nostrand Co. Inc., 1961).

5. Wayne Oates, *Religious Dimensions of Personality* (New York: Association Press, 1957).

6. See material on the work of Heinz Hartmann in Chap. 3.

7. Erik Erikson, *Childhood and Society* (New York: W. W. Norton & Co., 1963), 2nd ed., referred to below as "C & S"; Erikson, *Young Man Luther* (New York: W. W. Norton Co., 1958), referred to below as "YML"; Erikson, *Insight and Responsibility* (New York: W. W. Norton & Co., 1964), referred to below as "I & R"; Erikson, "Identity and the Life Cycle," Selected papers with a historical introduction by David Rapaport, in *Psychological Issues,* Vol. 1, No. 1, 1959 (New York: International Universities Press, Inc.), referred to below as "Issues."

8. Issues, pp. 55-65.

9. O. Spurgeon English and Gerald H. Pearson, *Emotional Problems of Living* (New York: W. W. Norton & Co., 1963), 3rd ed.; Ruth L. Munroe, *Schools of Psychoanalytic Thought* (New York: The Dryden Press, Inc., 1955); Calvin S. Hall and Gardner Lindzey, *Theories of Personality* (New York: John Wiley & Sons, Inc., 1957).

10. Anna Freud, *The Ego and Mechanisms of Defense* (New York: International Universities Press, 1946).
11. C & S, p. 194.
12. Issues, pp. 22-23.
13. Issues, p. 102.
14. Issues, p. 113.
15. Issues, YML, and I & R.
16. Issues, p. 30.
17. Issues, p. 30.
18. Issues, p. 31.
19. Issues, p. 52.
20. Issues, p. 52.
21. Issues, pp. 53-55.
22. Issues, p. 55.
23. Issues, p. 55.
24. Issues, p. 56.
25. Issues, p. 57.
26. Issues, p. 58.
27. Issues, p. 63.
28. Issues, p. 60.
29. Issues, pp. 60-61.
30. Issues, p. 63.
31. Issues, p. 61.
32. Issues, p. 64.
33. Issues, p. 65.
34. Issues, p. 68.
35. Issues, p. 70.
36. Issues, p. 71.
37. Issues, p. 76.
38. Issues, p. 76.
39. Issues, p. 79.
40. Issues, p. 80.
41. Issues, p. 81.
42. Issues, pp. 84-86.
43. Issues, p. 88.
44. Issues, p. 92.
45. Issues, p. 93.
46. YML, p. 43.
47. YML, p. 102.
48. Issues, p. 132.
49. Issues, p. 116.
50. Helen B. Carlson, M.D., Carl Christensen, M.D., Alfred Flarsheim, M.D., Bernard L. Greene, M.D., William Nolan, M.D., Erich Paschkes, M.D., Charles Schlageter, M.D., Julian Pathman, Ph.D. and Clara Weimer, Ph.D. "Diagnosis and Treatment of an Acute Confusional State in College Students." *Quarterly Bulletin,* Northwestern Uni-

versity Medical School. Chicago, 1958, Vol. 32, No. 1, p. 6.

51. Issues, p. 95.
52. Issues, p. 96.
53. Issues, p. 96.
54. Issues, p. 97.
55. Issues, p. 97.
56. Issues, p. 97.
57. Issues, p. 98.
58. C & S, p. 268.
59. Issues, p. 98.
60. Issues, p. 99.

Chapter 6. *The Making of a Pastor*

1. See Kurt Lewin, *Resolving Social Conflicts* (New York: Harper & Row, 1948), Chap. 4. Also, Carl Rogers, *Client-Centered Therapy,* (Boston: Houghton Mifflin Co., 1951), Chap. 9.
2. Erik Erikson, *Young Man Luther* (New York: W. W. Norton, Inc., 1958).
3. Margaretta Bowers, *Conflicts of the Clergy* (New York: Thomas Nelson & Sons, 1963).
4. Today certain groups are offering scholarships for young men who are not committed to the ministry to study in a theological seminary. Limited experience with such programs suggests that many of these students have identity needs which will never be resolved by a purely academic approach, and that these programs need to add a therapeutic dimension.

Index